£9.99

Celtic Lore and Druidic Ritual

By Rhiannon Ryall

GW00655977

Celtic Lore and Druidic Ritual

ISBN 1 898307 24 5

First printed 1994
Reprinted 1995 (twice)
Reprinted 1996
Reprinted 1997 (twice)

Cover design by Daryth Bastin
Cover illustration by Simon Rouse

Published by:

Capall Bann Publishing
Freshfields
Chieveley
Berks
RG20 8TF

Dedication

To my beloved daughter Rosemary, who was taken to live in the Isles of the Blest at twenty-eight years of age.

'Bismillahi ar Rahman ar Rahim'

(Quoted by nomadic Arabs when starting out on a long journey, an English translation is "in the name of Allah, the merciful, the compasssionate")

Also by Rhiannon Ryall and published by Capall Bann:

Weaving A Web of Magic (Celtic Lore Part 2)

West Country Wicca

Symbols of Ancient Gods

Teachings of the Wisewomen

Introduction

Having written *"West Country Wicca"*, which is primarily concerned with the overt/public face of Witchcraft, I feel the time has come to bring some of the Inner Mysteries to those interested in any Pagan Path or Tradition.

The Tradition I am describing has its roots in Western Ireland. Inevitably the Druidic Path crosses that of any genuine Gaelic Tradition of Witchcraft, so this book contains much Druidic lore. I have included some background material pertaining to the Druids, as this explains much of their way of viewing the world. It enables the reader to understand more fully their attitudes in general, and their Rituals in particular.

As this system in common with that of the Druids in one method of working, is based on the five-fold calendar, I have called the chapters or divisions of the book by the names of the Five Islands known to the Druids and the de Danaan Tradition of Witchcraft,as the realms where originally their knowledge was taught. This system places emphasis on the five days "outside of the year", and five Festivals of which Lady Day on 25th.March is one. The Druids have other ways of working, which include an eightfold and even a fortyfold calendar, but I have concentrated on the most widely used system, that of the fivefold.

One final comment; in *"West Country Wicca"*, I did include one small piece of "Inner Lore", but of all the thousands who bought the book, in various countries throughout the world, the only person to pick up this little hint, was a Druid living in the Eastern States of Australia. This in no small part prompted me to write this book, as evidently the Inner Knowledge is still largely unknown by what are called by Traditionalists, the "New Wave" Pagans.

"Among the pen friends which this book produced, were representatives of the old Witch religion. There are still some of these, who are quite distinct from the modern imitative covens...."

Professor T. C. Lethbridge, *"The Essential T. C. Lethbridge"* Edited by Tom Graves and Janet Hoult. Published by Routledge and Kegan Paul. London. 1980.

Contents

Chapter One

Fínías

A working area for a Druid is set up in virtually the same way as that of a Witch. In other words, it should be near oak trees and running water if possible. The Druids only work in groves of trees, using the trees to physically set the boundaries of the Circle. In Druidic terms, the Gorsedd, or Sacred Enclosure. Witches generally just prefer to have oak trees close at hand, as the polarity of oak is female. Both systems mark the Circle boundary in the same way, as follows:

The outline of the Circle, and it should be nine feet in diameter, or in multiples of nine, is outlined on the ground by a wand or sharp stick. A knife or sword should NEVER be used to dig in the ground, as it alters the earth energy. If by chance the Circle is on a ley line, it damages the energies of the line. The groove made by the stick should then be filled by rock or sea salt. The other materials that can be used to fill this groove, are chalk, mustard seeds, or quartz chips. The reason one of these materials are used, is that they act as a kind of "psychic blocker", and help to contain the energies raised within the Circle.

I am of the opinion that the use of these materials was originally only Druidic, and that it was passed on to the "Fertility Cult" peoples, who would have been the forerunners of the Witches. Of course I am speaking of a time several thousands of years ago. There have been Witches as such, for a very long time indeed, but their ancestors were probably groups of those who had a fertility cult. That the Druids had more "technology" for want of a better word, than did the original Witches is plain.

This use of a "psychic blocker", also assists in making the Circle a "place between the worlds", in which the Otherworld Beings or Archetypes can be invoked or evoked.

When the Circle has been marked with the salt or other material, FOUR fires are lit in the quarters but OUTSIDE the Circle boundary.

I realise that today it is often very difficult to light so many fires, so if it is really impossible, then four little lanterns can be used or even candles at a pinch, but ideally there should be four fires.

A fifth fire should also be lit but INSIDE the boundary for this one, and it should be in the NORTH EAST. This fire is known as the "Watchfire", and is most important so if it is impossible to light a fire on the ground, then a firepot should be used or even a cauldron. A Male Witch stands by this Watchfire, and he is known as the Circle Guardian. This Guardian plays a major role in many Rituals.

In times of persecution I think that this male Witch did literally keep watch for strangers, but that is NOT the original or prime reason for his role. Celtic Witchcraft is based on contact with Otherworld dwellers or Archetypes, whether they are in "Annwn" - the Underworld, or "Gwynfed" - the Blessed Realm, or Isles of the Blest, or Avalon, whatever title you choose to call it.

The Otherworld per se, consists of both Annwn and Gwynfed. Bran in ONE ASPECT ONLY, is Guardian of a Sacred Fire. This fire has a deep spiritual meaning, being one of the Inner Mysteries of Druidism, which I will not comment on at this time. The Male Witch who is the Circle Guardian of the Watchfire, represents on the physical plane the role of Bran in the Otherworld. I have tried to use a male who resembles the Light Aspect of Bran; auburn to gold hair, beard and moustache. This Watchfire Guardian also always wears a black robe.

6

The Circle Guardian is the origin I think, of the "New Wave" Wiccans, "Man in Black". I have attended a few "New Craft" Covens, and the Man in Black seems to me to be like a Director of a stage play. The real and vital meaning of his role completely unknown to the Coven members. This is the real problem with a lot of New Witchcraft, it has so much information missing, that it is like trying to make a good cake with only four out of seven ingredients. Which is one of the reasons for this book.

Incidentally, all Otherworld Archetypes or Deities have a Light and a Dark side. This is not dark as in evil, simply a "heavier" energy to work with. This Dark energy's polarity interestingly enough, is feminine. This polarity does not change, regardless of the season or condition of the Great Tides. It is only in things of the physical world, that the polarity changes at certain times.

As with all metaphysical work, balance is essential. Balance in the person working a Ritual, and balance in the type of Ritual. To work always with Light energies, means that one has a vast area of esoteric knowledge lost to one, and to work only the heavy energies, is also no good. One must experience both "Yin" and "Yang", to borrow an example from another culture. As one Archetype instructed me: "Without the Dark there would be no perception of Light. Without the dark earth to nourish its very rootrun there would be no Snowdrop blooming in its purity of whiteness, no Rose blossoming to perfume the air. Their very lifeblood emanates from the dark of the earth".

So for us, it is necessary in our spiritual quest to experience both.

Ritually pacing to a Circle, even if they have only just vacated it, helps to set the mood and the minds of the participants onto the magical work at hand.

The best way to enter the Circle and activate it, is with dance and "calls". I give the "calls" later on in this chapter. The dance can be of two varieties, whichever you feel on the night would be the most appropriate. A circling dance can be performed, with jumping and stamping down on alternate feet as one goes round the inner perimeter of the Circle. The Coven can join hands for this if they choose. Circling Deosil (clockwise) produces the well known "cone of power", circling Widdershins, (counter-clockwise), produces a vortex of power. The cone of power is masculine in polarity, the vortex of power is feminine in polarity. For balance, two circles of people can dance if there are enough participants. The males on the outer rim dancing Widdershins, the females inside the circle of male dancers, dancing Deosil.

The other method is for all to go in in single file, and circle in a spiral towards the middle of the Circle, then spiral out again towards the perimeter. These dances are only for activating a Circle as it were, there is still more to be done before it is truly ready to work in.

I will mention the well known "back to back" dance, but it is very difficult to carry out, even if the pairs of people are of similar height. One has a tendency to topple over, which rather spoils the effects one is trying to build! However, for those who may not be aware of this dance, it involves a man and a woman, as many couples as you can muster, and they dance around the Circle, first one way and then the other, with their arms linked and their backs together, so that one sex is looking into the Circle, while the other is gazing out. Sometimes the men, (if they are very robust), hoist the women onto their backs, and then back onto the ground again. It is all very difficult to do however, and I think that the other two dances are more suitable being easier to carry out. It symbolises facing the seen and unseen worlds simultaneously.

If the spiral dance is done to the middle and out again, the ideal turning is three and a half turns towards the centre of the Circle, and three and a half turns out again. This is because the earth energy spirals are in turns of three and a half. While dancing, all involved can point their knives at the Circle's edge and try to see the energy flowing out of the knife tip, enhancing the Circle's boundary. The energies are drawn upwards from the ground through the feet into the body and out through arm and hand to knife tip. At the same time, energies are drawn from above, down through head and shoulder into the arm and hand and out through the knife. You may visualise the boundary as a wall of light, but most people see it in a different way from one another.

Once the dance is completed either all or one of each sex, go around the Circle and trace the appropriate Sigil in each quarter. I list these at the end of the chapter, and also the appropriate woods for the wands with which you trace the Sigils.

When this has been done, you may wish to work with one of the elements. In which case you go to its quarter and call on that particular type of elemental, taking with you a symbol of that element. A bowl of water for the West, a candle or lantern for the South, smoking herbs for the East, a bowl of earth for the North.

One such call is as follows:

"Guardian (or Sprite) of Earth/Air/Fire/Water, (whichever you are calling), I call ye and charge ye and charm ye in token of thy stewardship".

When you say "token", hold aloft the symbol of the element you are holding. I know that nowadays most modern Witches call in all four elements starting in the East and ending in the North. There are several ways of doing this, and I list these too at the end of the chapter.

If it is a Full Moon you will want to bring the Goddess energy into the Circle. Before I describe this, I would like to quote the following: Frances Hitching in a book called "Earth Magic", (published by Cassell in 1976), says:

"The Yorkshire painter Monica English describes her visions of rituals attending such cult centres as Avebury which involves processional movements, chants and many fires:-

"The idea was deliberately to make the circle powerful by pouring out their own emotions, and they did it so efficiently that you can still feel it there now. But at the time it was all to do with the preparation for the entrance of the Goddess Queen.

The reverence in which she was held was enormous. The circle protected her, but somehow at the same time allowed the life force to enter her and be concentrated in her. All the ritual was to lead up to the great moment when she was possessed and made her pronouncements like an oracle.

It was to do with fertility of nature, the safety of the cattle, the welfare of the people, that sort of thing - the original witchcraft, the natural sort, not at all the invented witchcraft which is around today"."

Now I do not subscribe to all of the preceding quote, but in the main it is a very valid opinion. One of my disagreements concerns the person taking in the Goddess energy. In my view, any female Witch can do this, once they are experienced. But I do agree that it produces an altered state of consciousness when properly and correctly carried out. There are once again, several ways of accomplishing this.

One way is for another dance to be undertaken with "calls". Now calls for the most part, are vowels only. The importance of vowel sounds can be demonstrated quite clearly by looking at the Hebrew Alphabet and the Hebrew hidden names. There are no vowels included. This is not because there were none, that would be ridiculous, but the Tetragrammaton, the four lettered name of the Hebrew god, is a case in point. In English it is "JHVH", so it has become "Jehovah", but only because no one except possibly some senior Rabbi's, know what the missing vowels are.

So Witchcraft "calls" are all vowels strung together in certain ways. They also need to be trilled or vibrated when vocalised, it is the vibrations in the ether that makes them work.

"I-A-O", is one such call for the Goddess. The sounds have to be made "long". "I-I-I-Ay-Ay-Ay O-O-O-O", that sort of sound needs to be trilled. Another one is, "O-A-U-E-I". I realise that they may look ridiculous, but they do work, and are almost as old as Homo Sapiens.

All very old magical systems view the Universe as either being composed of, or covered by, a fine, silver web. Old Shamans considered they used strands of the web to proceed along when seeking Inner Planes knowledge. It was rather like following a paper trail, so that one could not get lost, but simply had to follow it back when returning.

This silver web vibrates to thought in a lesser degree, and to sounds in a greater. The vibrating of the web on particular parts, produces certain results. So trilling out sounds that are associated with the Goddess or the feminine energies, will vibrate on that part of the web where that particular energy resides.

The female Witch who is going to bring in the Goddess energy through her body, stands in the North facing into the Circle. She should stand as a five pointed star. When she goes into the trance, she will not be aware of her out-stretched arms, and so can maintain the position, while the Goddess energy holds her, and imparts whatever truths and insights the Coven is going to receive.

Now when this Witch takes up her position, the others may stand in a semi-circle in front of her and declaim:

"Behold! The Mystery of Mysteries;
The cloud before our eyes is lifting,
With love and joy our hearts and minds we bend
Towards that Power into our Priestess pouring,
O Gracious Goddess! From Thy Realm descend!"

While the Coven is reciting this, they may hold their knives in front of them, points towards the Priestess, or they may trace the following Sigil in front of her in the air:

This is a Sigil for Epona the Celtic Horse Goddess, but it does work very well, for the main Goddess energy.

The Gardnerian "Charge" that the female Witch recites in Gardnerian Witchcraft, is based on "Address to the Goddess", from Apuleius' book "The Golden Ass". Similarly, the sigils that some Witches have on their knife handles, are from the "Key of Solomon", as is the use of a white handled knife in addition to the black handled one.

There is nothing wrong with any of these things, but they are not Witchcraft. However, I do feel that reciting the "Charge", does negate the very effect being strived for, namely a state of light trance, but reciting it AFTER the empowerment by the Goddess, would not matter.

I am aware that I have not mentioned Sigils to be drawn in the quarters, but there are many, and I have included these also at the end of this chapter.

On a Full Moon night, most of the working is involved with bringing in the Goddess energy and receiving information from energies are not being used, they should be consciously poured back into the ground, to revitalise our Earth.

Cakes and wine have always ended a Circle Ritual, these can be placed near the cauldron, or in the North. On a Full Moon, the cakes and wine are held aloft, either together, with two people holding them, or separately. The Lady and Her Consort are thanked for them, and this phrase may be used at such a time:

"Great Lady and Mighty Lord, charge these the
fruits of the Earth, with love and understanding".

Now we come to the vexed question - at least nowadays - of ritual copulation. This generally takes place at a Full Moon, after empowerment by the Goddess. It is after all this has taken place, that any working is done, as the Ritual brings the life-force into the Circle. Any work done, should only be of a fertile nature, assisting the land if there is drought, or helping perhaps a couple who desire children, but seem unable to have them.

One of the problems with sex magic today is that times have changed. Also, like it or not, most people have been unconsciously "drilled" by nearly two thousand years of the Christian's morality. In addition, it seems at the present time, that Witchcraft is followed by many people who are not of a rural background, and they have not the acceptance of this very earthy side of living in a physical world, that many country folk still have. Also, sex magic was often carried out as a form of sympathetic magic, so that its use has rather fallen by the wayside.

The Druids use it to activate and recharge the energy spirals in the land. Druids are of both sexes. Most old Tradition people and that includes the Druids, who were taught as I was, are of the opinion that contrary to what most "modern" writers say, that it was a more effective Rite when carried out by two people who are NOT emotionally involved with each other.

This may sound rather outrageous perhaps even to Pagans, who, as I have stated, have nearly two millennia of Christian dogma in their cultural background.

The reasoning behind this viewpoint as stated, (and even the Inner Mysteries of Tibetan Buddhism are Tantric), is that the emotion two people feel for each other is likely to "get in the way" of the Ritual. This is because, (and this is NEVER mentioned in ANYONE'S books on Witchcraft), the two people involved, are supposed to ASTRALLY PROJECT FROM THEIR BODIES while the sex act is taking place. The man and the woman call down the respective God and Goddess forces within them before the Rite is carried out, and then they "go off". The physical bodies copulate, but the two people are NOT THERE. They "come back" at the conclusion.

In fact, this climactic of the life force, draws them back into their bodies. This is the reason why it should be impossible for pregnancy to occur. The two forces - Goddess and God - take the energy and use it for whatever magical purpose the Rite was intended. The only time that pregnancy would occur, was when the aim was a "magical child".

The one exception to this rule, is when Initiation is taking place. But even then, the INITIATOR astrally projects, only the person being Initiated does not.

The reason for astral projection is so that the Otherworld beings take over, so that this is NOT the sex act for enjoyment as in the everyday world, but a Rite of symbolic union of reconciling polarities; when it involves an Initiation, it is putting the Initiate in touch with the Otherworld power of the opposite gender, in the only way possible in a three dimensional world. A physical world at that.

However, times change and Witchcraft must also one assumes. If a married person enters the "Craft", and their partner does not, then probably only a symbolic union can take place. Then the Powers have to be called down and put into the two symbols of cup and knife or cup and wand. However, it should not be forgotten, that Witchcraft is the OLD Religion, and stems from a time when everyone was Pagan.

One of the problems pertaining to sexual matters is that we have endured for so long a society where people were made to feel there was something inherently wicked or sinful about sexual feelings. This caused many people particularly the young, to be plagued with guilts. Until recently, it had changed to a certain extent, but now, with the fear of catching an incurable, terminal illness, it is possible that the old, repressive attitudes will resurface, before many young people have been given a chance to reach maturity, in a more enlightened atmosphere.

However, I would like anyone who reads this book, to think carefully about my comments on the reasons for ritual sex. I think that what it should really be called is, "a spiritual magic engendered through the agency of the human body". But it is a rather unwieldy phrase.

But, back to the Full Moon Rite. How you finish the Ritual depends on those taking part. However, when everyone is ready to leave, the Guardian of the Watchfire calls "Fare-Well" to the Otherworld beings, including any elementals you may have called up. He then puts out the Watchfire. Now because this fire plays such an important part in Celtic Ritual, the fire needs extinguishing in a certain way.

By the end of the evening, the Guardian can have let the fire die down to red embers. He can disperse these a little, to encourage them to die out, but he extinguishes the fire with bunches of GREEN, NOT dried, Dwale. As he puts this on the remains of the fire, he says, "I return this fire to Annwn". (Dwale is deadly nightshade, Atropa Belladonna).

The outside fires may be put out in any way that is suitable. Covered with earth, or stamped on if they are really low. If you have used candles instead of the quarter fires, they can be put out and taken with you. The herbs that have burned in the quarters, should be sprinkled on the ground in their own quarter. The cauldron water should be tipped out in the middle of the Circle.

The Sigils that I give later on for the quarters, do not have to be taken down unless I so state. I give this information at the end of the chapter, with all the lists.

I have not mentioned an Altar, as it is not necessary to have one. One of the Inner Mysteries of Witchcraft is that only in Ritual copulation is an Altar used, and then the woman is the Altar.

However, if you want to use one, it should be put in the middle of the Circle, with the cauldron on it. Generally the only time a fire was lit in the middle of the Circle was for Handfasting, though one or two other Rites call for it. So if you have a fire in the

middle, then put the Altar in the North. To a Witch, that is where the power emanates from.

This Altar should be an Earth Altar, i.e., the height of an average persons solar plexus. All psychic energy stems from the solar plexus. An interesting fact is that the apex of the Great Pyramid is 76 degrees, and the apex of a human rib cage is 76 degrees. The Great Pyramid must have been constructed to use earth energies in some way.

If your Circle is on a permanent site, you will find its energies grow stronger and stronger the more you use it. If you wish, when using a cauldron in the middle of the Circle, you may draw the Circle using multiples' of the cauldron's diameter. The Druids often use this method, particularly if they are doing work with the cauldron. They have quite a lot of ritual and magical work which involves using the cauldron.

Sigils

The most famous sigil is I suppose, the pentagram or FIVE pointed star. This is in itself a very powerful working tool, as it is two ancient Celtic (Welsh) Runes joined together to spell out an old God Name. It is put together like this:

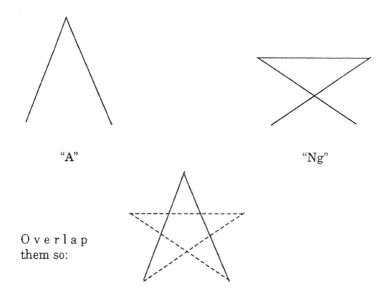

"A"

"Ng"

O v e r l a p
them so:

You now have the five pointed star. I have used a broken line for "Ng", simply in order to make it easier to see how Runes overlap. This old god is "Ang" or "Ing". The latter is slightly later spelling of the name. There are still Priests of Ang, but I do not know if there are any outside the British Isles. I list the Welsh Runes overleaf for any who may be interested. They are from the old Welsh book, "Barddas". This spelling is known as the "God form in the Pentagram".

40 Welsh Runes from "Barddas"

A ∧		MH ᛖ
B ∨		R ᚱ
V ᚼ		RH ᚼ
C ⟨		S ᚱ
CH ᚴ		Q ᚴ
NGH ᚴ		T ↑
D ⟩		TH ᚦ
DD ᚦ		NH ∣↑
E ⟪		FF ᚠ
F ᚠ		W ↓
G ᚄ		Y ⟩
NG ᚷ		GH ᚼ
H ┼		X ᚷ
I ∣		Z Z
L ᚴ		Â ∧
U Ν		Ê ∨
M ᚻ		Ô ◊
N ∩		Û ᚤ
O ◊		Y ᚤ
P ᚱ		PH .ᚼ

It will probably be noticed that some of these Runes are the same as the Germanic ones. Most Runes do seem to have the "arrow" shape for the letter "T", regardless of origin.

19

The Great Tides

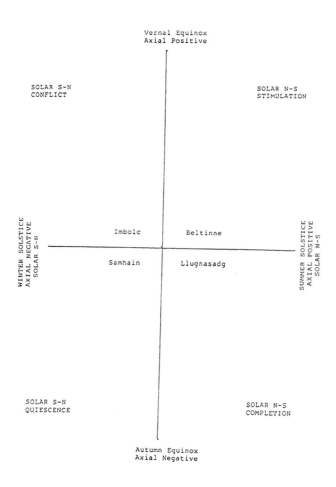

Vernal Equinox
Axial Positive

SOLAR S-N
CONFLICT

SOLAR N-S
STIMULATION

WINTER SOLSTICE
AXIAL NEGATIVE
SOLAR S-N

Imbolc   Beltinne

Samhain   Llugnasadg

SUMMER SOLSTICE
AXIAL POSITIVE
SOLAR N-S

SOLAR S-N
QUIESCENCE

SOLAR N-S
COMPLETION

Autumn Equinox
Axial Negative

Any new magical undertaking should be started from the Spring Equinox to the Summer Solstice.

Work which produces results on the physical Plane, Summer Solstice to Autumn Equinox.

Works which culminate in spiritual results, Autumn Equinox to Winter Solstice.

Works of withdrawal and contemplation, Winter Solstice to Spring Equinox.

It will be seen that the four Festivals are in between the times when the Tides change. They are the four "cross quarter days", on which the year hung, although originally, only Beltinne and Samhain were recognised and celebrated.

The Lunar Tides can be taken into account when working with the Great Tides, and I give them here for the Northern Hemisphere:

Lunar tides correspond with the phases of the Moon and change four times a month.

The Full Moon has the greatest power, and the Harvest Moon is the most powerful of the Full Moons.

The first quarter of a Moon is allied with inception and growth.

The New Moon is most magical in the Spring.

Sigils for the Thirteen Moons of the Year

These Sigils are used by the Druids in addition to some other Celtic Traditions, and they are connected with the thirteen consonants of the Ogham. They are all drawn from a Master Sigil known as the "Ogham Key". It was discovered so long ago that I cannot put a date to it, that all these Sigils and these only, could be drawn from the Ogham Key, without retracing any line, or having to break off and restart. It is similar in that regard to the Norse Runes. They are all taken from the "Hailstone" glyph in an identical manner.

The Oghams are not simply an alphabet, but are an integral part of a whole system, with a wealth of correspondences and uses. In this book, I will include as much of this information as I am allowed to.

All the Sigils are drawn Deosil and I have shown them as Lunar Invoking. It will be seen that the twenty-third of December is missing from the dates; that is because it was a "day outside of the year" the twenty-second being viewed as having forty hours in it not twenty four. This is related to the fact that all magical children are born at the Winter Solstice, and it is part of the ceremonies attending this event that the forty hours is used.

The vowels are not included. Apart from their mystical use, they also represent the Five Festivals that are celebrated by the Pagan Druids, and indeed by my own Celtic Tradition of Witchcraft.

These Five Festivals Are: Lady Day in March, Beltinne, Summer Solstice, Samhain and the Winter Solstice.

22

Dec. 24th. - Jan. 20th
Colour: White Feathers
Wand: Birch Wood
Bird Ogham: Pheasant
Herb: Mullein

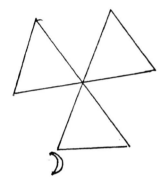

Jan. 21st - Feb. 17th
Colour: Floodwater Grey
Wand: Rowan
Bird Ogham: Duck
Herb: Rue

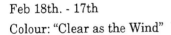

Feb 18th. - 17th
Colour: "Clear as the Wind"
Wand: Ash
Bird Ogham: Snipe
Herb: Herb Robert

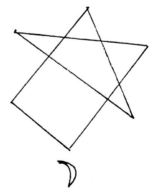

23

Mar. 18th - Apr. 14th
Colour: Crimson
Wand: Alder
Bird Ogham: Gull
Herb: Celandine

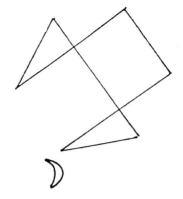

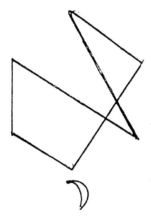

Apr. 15th. - May 12th.
Colour: Grass Green
Wand: Willow
Bird Ogham: Hawk
Herb: Mugwort

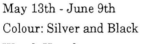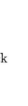

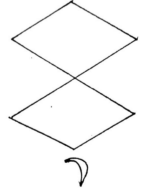

May 13th - June 9th
Colour: Silver and Black
Wand: Hawthorn
Bird Ogham: Crow
Herb: Chamomile

24

June. 10th - July 7th
Colour: Charcoal Black
Wand: Oak
Bird Ogham: Wren
Herb: Rosemary

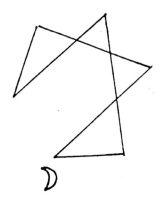

July 8th. - Aug. 4th
Colour: Iron Grey
Wand: Holly
Bird Ogham: Starling
Herb: Comfrey

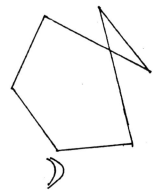

Aug. 5th. - Sept. 1st
Colour: Brown
Wand: Hazel
Bird Ogham: Crane
Herb: Nutmeg

Sep. 2nd. - Sept. 29th
Colour: Titmouse (Brown
            and Black)
Wand: Vine
Herb: Yarrow
Bird Ogham: Titmouse

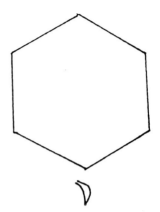

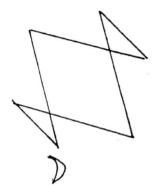

Sep. 30th. - Oct. 27th
Colour: Blue Smoke
Wand: Ivy
Bird Ogham: Mute Swan
Herb: Sage

Oct. 28th. - Nov. 24th
Colour: Sea Green
Wand: Reed or Water Elder
Bird Ogham: Goose
Herb: Vervain

Nov. 25th. - Dec. 22nd
Colour: Blood Red
Wand: Elder
Bird Ogham: Rook
Herb: Heather

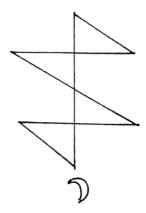

As these are Lunar Invoking, the commencement of the Sigil is from that point.

Wands of the pliable plants, may be twisted together or plaited to strengthen them.

The colours are rather different from normal descriptions, because they are from a time when all colours were taken from nature.

Calling Quarters

These particular ones are good at a New Moon. I have been told they are Druidic, but have not verified this yet. However, I have found that they work, so really that is all that matters.

EAST: Kernunnus! Of the twelve tines!
                    I do call thee up to attend this Rite!

SOUTH: Epona! White Mare of the Hills!
                    I do call thee up to attend this Rite!

WEST: Mona! Sacred cow of the Blessed Isle!
                    I do call thee up to attend this Rite!

NORTH: Artor! Great Bear! Lord of Logres!
                    I do call thee up to attend this Rite!

After using these quarters for a while, you will find that two male and two female warriors will appear, instead of the animals. These quarters can be dismissed as suggested in the section on Full Moon nights.

These quarters are for an "Earth" Ritual in particular, but can be used as a general method of quarters if desired.

You Will Need

A pot of earth for the North.

A pot of burning herbs for the East.

A candle or lantern for the South.

A pot of water for' the West-Rain water of course.

The herbs in the pot should be mugwort. If you wish, you may also burn the appropriate seasonal herbs in all four quarters.

Use a wand of Oak, and pointing it at the element while standing in that element's quarter, say:

"Air of Earth I charge thee with the Power of the Old Ones.

Fire of Earth I charge thee with the Power of the Old Ones.

Water of Earth I charge thee with the Power of the Old Ones.

Earth of Earth I charge thee with the Power of the Old Ones."

The Sigils drawn in the quarters would be the ones applicable for the time of year.

This is a system of tracing Sigils in the quarters, that was given me from another Tradition. The Pentagram is of course familiar, and in this case is drawn as an "earth" Pentagram. The other Sigils are reminiscent of the Druidic ones, another case no doubt of systems overlapping.

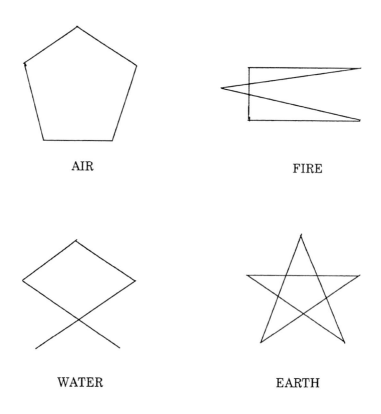

AIR

FIRE

WATER

EARTH

Dancing deosil produces a cone, dancing widdershins produces a vortex. One of the reasons for widdershins movements being viewed as "bad", is I believe partly a Christian overlay, in that the early Christians were anti-female, and some Pagan groups also, because the "heavy" energies that were worked by the pre-de-Danaan Covens, are worked with a vortex and not a cone.

Some Traditions of course, still work as the early Megalithic peoples did, and their work is with vortex energies, particularly as they work the "Dark Moon" cycle of the Goddess.

Male energy moves from above to below, from sky to earth. Female energy moves from below to above, from earth to sky. Male energy moves from the centre to the circumference of the Circle, female energy moves from the circumference to the centre. A cone is an outward moving, clockwise spiral of energy that is gold and white in colour.

A vortex is an inward moving anti-clockwise spiral of energy that is silver and black in colour.

A symbol for the cone is:

A symbol for the vortex is:

Some woods when made into wands will alter the polarity of the human body. Thus a male homosexual, who is to himself a woman, can produce feminine energy in his body, by holding a wand of elm wood. (All the preceding information is from notes taken at a lecture given by a senior Druid).

A pendulum that has a different swing for men and for women, can be used to discover the polarities of substances.

Here are some examples:

Male energy or polarity.	Female energy or polarity
Amber	Jet
Ash Wood	Oak wood
Rubies	Iron
Sunlight	Moonlight

From this list it can be seen that the traditional Witches necklace of Amber and Jet, is perfectly balanced in its polarity. In all, there are three substances which will change the polarity of a person. Elm wood as I have mentioned previously, plus graphite and charcoal

Apart from polarities looked at in this particular way, it should also be born in mind that layers of organic and inorganic materials work better than just one kind on its own. That is why a Witches' knife should have a wooden handle, because of the metal blade. Even when the knife has a blade of bronze which is the traditional material, it should still have a wooden handle.

In the days of knights in armour, the knights helmets were often lined with straw, which gave the layers again. The armour also had some little knobs on the inside, which pressed against various acupuncture points to keep their vitality at a high level. Some of the traditional headbands worn by Druids, have knots in them that fit on the temple areas of the forehead.

The round shields of wood, trimmed with an iron rim were also designed in that way for the reasons of having a balanced polarity. The measurements of round shields was very complicated, and was based on the Planetary orbits in the heavens.

There is still a huge body of information and knowledge connected with the manufacture of ancient weaponry, but apart from its general interest, it is not a great deal of use to us today, so I will leave the subject there for the present.

The sword is a comparatively new magical weapon to Witchcraft, although it has always figured in Druidic workings and some other Celtic Paths. The mix of organic and inorganic materials is rather difficult with a sword, but what it should have is a pommel of copper. Iron being female and copper male.

With regards to copper, there are books on the market that tell you how to make magical weapons of copper and crystals. One shows a copper wand crystal tipped and encased in leather. Now this is fine as far as it goes, but to make it really work well and efficiently, you need to pack the inside of the copper tube with alternate layers of organic and inorganic materials.

I have found that the easiest way of doing this, is to put in alternate layers of bits of sheep fleece and some small stones. You do this until the tube is full. The best way of getting the wool in, is to ram it down the tube with a knitting needle. The little stones just drop in.

If everything is done correctly, and this includes Circle setting up and working, the results produced are very gratifying. Although this is not the main reason of course, for wanting good results.

The main reason, or perhaps the ONLY reason, for doing everything correctly, right Sigils, herbs, colours and chants, is that when an Otherworld persona is then called in for help or advice, that deity is without doubt present for all to be aware of, and listening. I cannot emphasis enough, the amount of energy generated in a Circle when it has been built with old, valid knowledge, in comparison with a Circle that has been put up with all the intent and goodwill in the world, but WITHOUT knowledge.

I still emphasise though, that you need to work outdoors away from the noise of modern life, and without the confines of four walls and a ceiling. This is to me the tragedy of so-called "Modern Craft"; it is so far removed from its rootstock, no fires, sticks of commercial incense, setting up in living rooms, elaborate altars, covered in statuary, this brings nothing EXTRA to the Ritual at all. It can drain power away in fact, or at best, detract from it.

Ceremonial Magicians work in indoor Temples, some of them are very good at it too - but it is not Witchcraft. Witches work outdoors with the things of nature. So if you want to work indoors - be a Magician!

Which brings me to "Regalia". Robes are useful. The climate does not always allow for working nude, and in any case, many old Witches did not. The main times it is necessary, and this has always been so, is at some Initiations and when Tantric magic is being worked. Although again, it depends on the type of Magic. Empowerment by the Goddess Energy, what is now popularly called "Drawing Down the Moon", (although strictly speaking it is only the Mediterranean areas that actually DO "Drawing Down the Moon"), can be done either way.

One of the arguments for robes, is weather, and some Witches are of the opinion that their robes gather energy from constant use. The wearing of robes in Britain is traditional for two main reasons. One is the aforementioned weather, the other is that on dark nights, wearing robes makes the person very hard to see. This probably stems from the times of persecution. The Druids of course, always wear robes, but the colour of them denotes their Degree. It is the Christian Druids that wear white, meet at Stonehenge and so forth, NOT the Pagan Druids.

Robes of earth colours are best, brown, very dark blue, green, or even black. They need only be plain, and the Kaftan shape is easy to make and wear. The robe is traditionally sewn by its wearer, and sewn by hand, so the Caftan is easiest if making it in this time-honoured way.

A necklace of acorns is also very traditional, although I have in addition to my acorn one, a necklace of glazed pottery in small saucer like shapes, threaded on leather. This particular necklace was made as a gift to me by a Witch I had helped in her personal life, so I wear it in gratitude to its giver, and it is anyway a very appropriate shape.

The acorn necklaces do need to be replaced every so often, as the acorns eventually dry up and split. They should be buried in the Circle when this happens, never just discarded.

A cord is useful to hang one's knife on, and it should be four and a half feet long, so that it can be used to draw a nine foot Circle. Some Celtic traditions use red, black and white cords plaited together. These are the three colours of the stones used in the buildings of Atlantis. The Druids have this and other explanations for the colours, but their other reasons are part of their Inner Mysteries.

I was told that green, silver and gold could be used, or a mix of these colours. The cord can have knots in it, for various reasons. If you wish to do a knot charm for yourself, then the knots could be put in the cord, but then that set of knots is there permanently. Our year is divided into forty working times, so the cord has forty knots in it.

There is a lot of rubbish talked about the Witches knife. It is an extension of yourself, so if you were going to put some plants in your garden, how much more energy would be given the plant if your knife was used to dig the hole, instead of a garden trowel?

I realise that I have warned about iron and ley lines, but that is mainly when casting a Circle, where no interruption in the energy is vital. Also, most garden implements are metal anyway, so I still think your own knife will add more to the plant. If it is not made of iron or steel, then that is a great bonus.

The Witches knife does not have to be treated like some hallowed or sacred object, it is a working tool, that is used for magic in addition to more homely tasks. The Witch herself or himself is a magical working tool in a way, but it does not preclude us from everyday mundane tasks. Witchcraft is of nature and is an earthy philosophy. In the main, I tell people that if it feels right to them, then that is the way to go. It is a Mystery Religion to the extent that it is a Hidden Path, but it does not need Mystique. Incidentally, I do not like the word "religion" when speaking of this old Path, as I feel it is more a philosophy - a way of life - than ever it is of being just a religion.

We try to bring together in the physical world, the real and True counterpart of this life, which is always there but unseen, so in the Circle, we try to get a little way from the physical world and a little way towards the Otherworld, so that they can overlap and interact in a positive, beneficial way, for all the participants.

A small thought to conclude this chapter, which has concerned itself in part with polarity and spiral energy. We live on the end of a spiral in a spiral shaped galaxy. Our Planet has spirals of energy within it. Women have a spiral of energy in the vagina. "As above, so below but after another manner".

Old Celtic/Irish form of oath-keeping. The deity names of tribes were kept secret:

Chapter Two

Falías

The "Festivals" have always been fairly public occasions. The main reason being that to work serious Ritual at these times, most old Traditions either use the older calendar, or as in the case of the Druids, they go by the Degrees of the Zodiacal Signs. Again, this means that they work Ritual after the night that is overtly accepted as Beltinne, Samhain, or whatever.

The Summer and Winter Solstices were worked at either dawn or dusk of the relevant nights. This is not always the same date each year, once again. Beltinne and Samhain have particular Hidden Rites attached to them, and generally these are celebrated anything up to twelve days after the "public" date of the Festivals.

Lady Day was not generally viewed as a public festival, so the magical work done was usually undertaken on the 25th March. This is the only festival with a "fixed" date, and presumably in the old calendar, the actual date would have been earlier than March 25th. The Tradition I was taught did not celebrate the two Equinox. They were simply acknowledged in passing as the first day of Spring and the first day of Autumn.

One reason for this omission may be suggested by T.G.E. Powell in his book *"The Celts"*, published in 1958 by Thames and Hudson. He says, "The possibility should always be born in mind that Imbolc may have been originally peculiar to some one cultural or occupational population group.

That Lughnasad was a festival introduced in name if not in purpose, by a late-coming group of settlers to Ireland seems well indicated in the stories connected with the god Lug. This festival seems to be the most agrarian in character of those known from Ireland. Its date, the first of August, does not accord well with a pastoralist economy when summer transhumance would have been in full swing. The god Lug is portrayed in the mythological tracts as a late-comer to the society of Irish divine beings of less archaic character than the others".

I would emphasise, that Beltinne and Samhain from a Celtic view-point would be the most significant times, with the Winter Solstice hardly any less significant.

With regard to Lady Day, that the Druids recognise and celebrate this is well established. At the 1974 Wexford Festival in Ireland, the Wexford Arts Centre was officially opened. Part of the official ceremonies, was a lecture given by Mr. Lawrence Durdin-Robertson, on Goddess worship. He enumerated the perpetual festivals, among which was Lady Day. Druids of my acquaintance celebrate Lady Day.

The Fivefold system is based on two concepts: One is the five pointed star representing the four elements and the Other-world. The second is the four islands where the de Danaans were taught their magical knowledge, and the fifth Sacred Isle.

So as there are already many books available to explain how to celebrate the Festivals in their overt form, I will not add to their numbers, but instead will explain Rituals for some of them that are carried out up to twelve days later and are of a more arcane nature.

First however I will explain about the four Islands of the Tuatha de Danaan, and their attributions. Each island has a Magical Weapon symbolising it. These are slightly different from the magical weapons now generally referred to. The original Celtic Magical Weapons are as follows:

Island of Finias: Fire, South, SPEAR
Island of Falias: Earth, North, SHIELD
Island of Murias: Water, West, CAULDRON
Island of Gorias: Air, East, SWORD

The Sacred Isle has a particular type of stone as its Magical Weapon, but I will not go into detail about this at this point. I will say however, that this is the Magical Weapon now known as the GRAIL. It is NOT a cup, or: chalice at all, but this special Stone.

In modern times, the Shield has become the Pentacle, the Cauldron the Goblet or Chalice, and the Spear and the Sword which are both in the de Danaan and Druidic Traditions, have in some instances, vanished altogether.

Much of Witchcraft at present, seems to have many bits of ceremonial magic in it, as for example, the pentacle, but if there was at one time no information freely available of these things, it is not surprising.

As I have said before, if a Thing works and works well, it really does not matter about its source, but often bits of different systems knitted together, do not always bring very startling results. The only yardstick to measure by, is does it bring extra energies into a Circle, that can be perceived by all? Does it amplify the Circle to give a Rite its full blown power?

At the end of this chapter I have listed the names of the thirteen Moon months, purely as a matter of interest, but here I will list the Five Festivals, their appropriate woods for wands, herbs, etc. Incidentally the wands throughout this book are for tracing the quarter Sigils in the air.

LADY DAY: Element: Water
                      Magical Weapon: Cauldron
                      Wood: Willow
                      Herb: Lady's Mantle
                      Vowel: "O"

BELTINNE: Element: Fire
                      Magical Weapon: Wand
                      Wood: Hazel
                      Herb: Celandine
                      Vowel: "A"

MIDSUMMER: Element: Earth
                      Magical Weapon: Cords
                      Wood: Oak
                      Herb: Rue
                      Vowel: "U"

SAMHAIN: Element: The Otherworld
                      Magical Weapon: Stone
                      Wood: Elder
                      Herb: Clover
                      Vowel: "E"

YULE: Element: Air
                      Magical Weapon: Knife
                      Wood: Rowan
                      Herb: Mugwort
                      Vowel: "I"

Quarters - Lady Day & Midsummer

These quarters were often drawn with staves instead of wands, but wands would be perfectly acceptable. There is another reason for these Sigils, which is explained in the appropriate chapter of this book.

When using these Sigils in the quarters, one person need not trace them all. Four people may draw one each, or two people do two each. It is a matter of choice.

So you will need:

> ACORNS for the NORTH
> HAZEL NUTS for the SOUTH
> BIRCH LEAVES for the EAST
> WILLOW LEAVES for the WEST

You can gather all these in the Autumn, and then store them until the right time for use. If you store the leaves in jars, you will need to label them, because when they dry out you may not be able to tell which is which. They may also be picked green and preserved but that is a lot more complicated. You will also need FOUR WANDS, one each of BIRCH, HAZEL, WILLOW, and OAK. These are for tracing the Sigils.

When casting the Circle, you can either use the herbs and Sigils for the time of year, and then do these afterwards, or you can substitute these for the seasonal ones. However, I have found that if you use both, the Circle energies are very much stronger, but it depends on what you wish to do.

Having put the acorns, nuts and leaves in the correct quarters, commencing in the East, you now take up the Birch wand to trace that quarters Sigil. You go round deosil from the East, finishing in the North.

Trace in the East the following Sigil:
at the same time saying:
"In the East the silver streams".

Trace in the South the following Sigil:
at the same time saying:
"In the South the Fire gleams

Trace in the West the following Sigil:
at the same time saying:
"In the West the boughs lean down".

Trace in the North the following Sigil:
at the same time saying:
"In the North the quarters Crown".

When the Ritual is over, the wands should be kept. Depending on the condition of acorns, nuts and leaves whether you decide to keep them or not. If you decide not to, they should be buried in the Circle. These Sigils do not need to be banished.

I have been told that these Sigils are also used in Orkney Island Witchcraft, which was a piece of news that came as a surprise to me, but as the Orkney Islanders are of Celtic origins, I suppose it is not all that remarkable.

The following Ritual can be carried out at either Lady Day or Midsummer, and it concerns bringing in an additional 1, mix of male and female energies. This can be poured into the ground to add to the earth's vitality, it can be poured into a new magical weapon for consecration purposes, it can be used to assist with healing someone. The objective is entirely up to the participants.

The Ritual only needs four people to work it, and that is one of the reasons I have included it, as I know that often there is not a full Coven available.

The Circle is cast in the usual way. If you have stones at the quarters, you may see them glow at the peak of the Rite.

A woman stands in the North, with another in the South. A man stands in the East, with another in the West. The women draw MASCULINE energy into the Circle, the men draw in FEMININE energy. All four direct it to the centre of the Circle.

Now they all move round, still concentrating, and the two women stand where the men stood, and the two men where the women stood. This time, the WOMEN draw the FEMININE energy, and the MEN the MASCULINE energy. It is still directed at the middle.

All four now move towards the centre until they can hold hands. With concentration, they will see four twisting channels of energy, which bunch together at the base. They then direct this to whatever work they have decided on.

Ritual Dance for Beltinne or Midsummer

This dance is for only four people again, but a fifth person is also involved. The fifth person who has to be a woman, stands in the North and chants. This Ritual can also be used at the Full Moon, or for charging a knife.

It is an Invocation to the Goddess, recited by the woman in the North, while the other four, two men and two women, perform a dance with wands and knives. The wands should be of Hawthorn wood - a Goddess tree.

First of all, here is the Invocation to be chanted. This Witch standing in the North, holds her knife in her right hand, and with arm upright, points it to the sky.

The Call of Nine

"I stand before Thy throne
I invoke Thee alone
I hold aloft my blade
Descend! As the spell is made
Lend the Power to give it life
The Power into my knife
On earth, in sky and shining sea,
O Gracious Goddess be with me
Come now the Call is made
Give Thy Power unto my blade"

The four people who dance, hold the wands in their left hands, knives in the right. They dance individually around the Circle, but keeping their movements synchronised. They do one movement for each line, EXCEPT LINE SEVEN, which has two movements with it. Here is a diagram of the dance, with descriptions of the movements.

MOVEMENT ONE:
Knife hand up, wand hand down,
right leg bent at knee.

MOVEMENT TWO:
Wand hand up, knife hand down,
left leg bent at knee.

MOVEMENT THREE:
Both arms up, bent at elbows,
accompanied by a leap in the air.

MOVEMENT FOUR:
Both arms straight up in the air,
and a sideways leap deosil.

MOVEMENT FIVE:
Both arms straight out from the sides,
a high step around, going deosil.

MOVEMENT SIX:
Both arms crossed over ribs, a
pause with feet still.

MOVEMENT SEVEN:
Knife arm stretched out straight in
front, other arm bent towards body,
a step with one leg high, going
Widdershins.

MOVEMENT EIGHT:
Both arms bent at elbows, facing
forwards together, palms facing in,
another sideways leap Widdershins.

MOVEMENT NINE:
Both arms overhead, wand and knife
touching. Another sideways leap
Widdershins, as previously.

COMPLETION:
Stand with arms down at sides.

There are two Rites of Evocation that can be carried out at
Samhain and Yule. One is for the Summoning of Herne, the
Leader of the Wild Hunt, and one is for Summoning the
Otherworld Guardian of the Watchfire to the Circle.

The best time to summon the Guardian is at Samhain, when of
course traditionally, the door between the worlds swings on its
hinges. It is the Old Celtic New Year.

Herne is essentially an Autumnal or winter type of figure so the
best time to summon him is at Yule - the Winter Solstice.

I have contacted him at other times of the year, but I think it is because I have been contacting him for a very long time, that has something to do with it.

I will explain the Ritual for Herne first, but before I do, I will quote this extract from the British Folk-Lore Society, as it is rather interesting: "The Yell Hounds, or ghost pack, were heard pattering through Stogumber after midnight this year, but no one looked out to see them, even nowadays. They are known to run through the village and down towards Roebuck, then on up to Willsneck". (Reported 1960. R. L. Tongue, "Somerset Folklore", Ed.K.Briggs. The Folklore Society, County Folklore.vol.viii.1965).

The village of Stogumber is between the Quantock hills, and Exmoor Forest. So the place referred to as "Willsneck", would be a high point on Exmoor. I do not actually know the point mentioned, but it is probably a very local name for it. However, it does show that even in the days of sophisticated technology, there are others apart from Witches, who still believe in things that pertain to the Old Ways.

A word of warning; NEVER summon an Otherworld person or Archetype unless you have a very good reason. While they are basically friendly and well disposed to those of the human race who are aware of them, they do not expect to be called simply to see if it "really works".

There are certain facial characteristics with Herne, that leave one in no doubt as to whether a summoning is actually him. Also his hounds do not make the same noises that ordinary dogs do. They have a distinctive cry of their own. I will not explain these peculiarities, but you will know yourself if you have raised him and his hounds.

If I explain it all you may think it your imagination when he is called. But if I do not give details and you see the differences for yourself, you will know you are successful.

Apart from the different noise, Herne's hounds behave exactly like the dogs of our world - if it doesn't move - they urinate on it!

Bearing all this in mind, here is one of the Rites for Summoning Herne and his Hounds.

You need a green shield. This can be green painted cardboard, or thin wood. It need not be very large, about eighteen inches high by twelve inches wide will do. It needs to be the following shape:

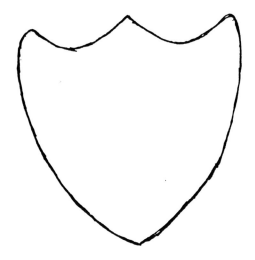

The green this is painted should be a fairly light shade, a sort of spring green, not dark. It should also have two spirals on it, a right handed one and a left handed one. Between the spirals, are two diamond like shapes. All need to be gold in colour. I have found the easiest way to do this is to use thick, gold coloured wool, and glue it to the shield with white glue. To do the diamonds, white card can be cut to shape and painted with gold paint, then also glued on. Below is a diagram of how it should look when it is finished.

Diagram of the completed shield:

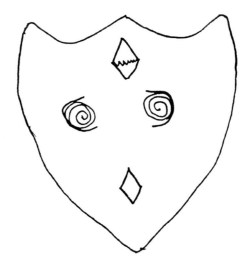

The top diamond shape represents an acorn. This shield needs to be propped up in the North quarter of the Circle. Then you will need one green candle and one gold candle in each of the quarters. A total of four candles in each colour. You will not need the fires outside the Circle in the quarters, but you will need the Watchfire. Or, you can light a fire in the cauldron in the middle of the Circle. In which case, the Circle diameter must be based on the diameter of the cauldron.

On the fire and in the herb pots for the quarters, you will need to burn a mixture of Mugwort, Wormwood, Horehound, Violet Root, and Wild Parsley.

Wood for the fire should be a mix of rowan, fir, and ash. Place acorns in the North, oak leaves in the South, vine leaves in the

West, and ivy leaves in the East.

Four horse shoes should be placed around the centre of the Circle, open ends pointing inwards. They should have white hairs from a horses tail threaded through them, but if this is not possible, then the plant known as "Mare's Tail", can be used instead.

The Circle is cast in the usual way, and when that is done, throw a good handful of the mixed herbs on the fire. Everyone should now stand in the North area. The Circle Guardian of course, would be there anyway.

All then declaim:

> *"I walked among the Nine*
> *With the Stones fair standing;*
> *On the borders of Time,*
> *Twixt Acorn and Oak leaf,*
> *Twixt Vine and Ivy."*

Now go to each quarter in turn, starting in the East and moving deosil. The Guardian blows a hunting horn three times at each quarter, then everyone calls:

> *"Awake Old Herne!*
> *Awake and ride!*
> *Come to the Call!*
> *Ride! Master! Ride!*
> *Awake to the Call!"*

The horn is blown three times in each quarter again after the Call. When all this has been carried out, and he has not manifested, all dance deosil around the Circle, while still blowing the horn. Look at all the quarters, as I have known him appear in the West and the North, on two different occasions. Like an absolute idiot, I did not think to make a note of the differences in the two nights time of year, phase of the Moon etc.

When he has manifested and answered your questions, thank him and bid him farewell in a positive way, so that he is in no doubt that you have finished.

It is best to close the Circle immediately afterwards. No wine or cakes. Take everything out of the Circle with you as well. You may burn the leaves and acorns, but make sure nothing is left in the Circle. The Watchfire Guardian still puts out the fire in the usual way, even if it is in the cauldron.

I have always found Herne to be friendly but very earthy. His hands look as if he spends his time grubbing up roots with them, and he smells a bit like old compost, but he is concerned in a practical way with the well being of our Planet. I always enjoy meeting Herne, partly I suppose because I come from a part of the world, where he is an everyday sort of energy to the residents. Incidentally, the village of Stogumber that was quoted in the extract from the British Folklore Society, has an inn called the "White Horse". Quite a significant name if Herne is a local resident as it were!

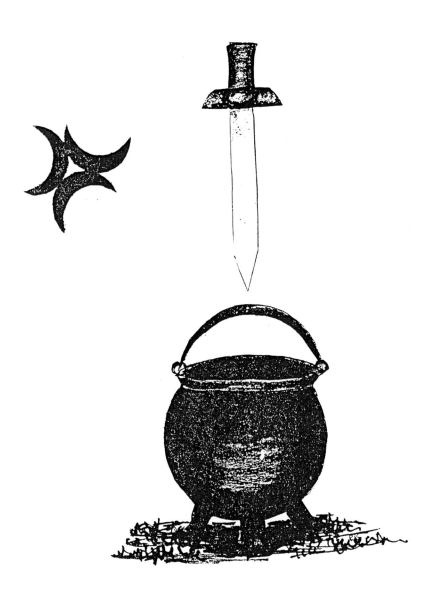

Summoning Bran

Summoning the Guardian, or Bran, should also not be undertaken unless the NEED is there. This applies even more in this instance, than it does to Herne.

This Ritual is undertaken at Samhain, when the Otherworld is very close, so in some ways, it is an easier Evocation than that of Herne.

The Circle is cast in the usual way, the Watchfire is laid, but NOT LIT, as you will need to build a little barrow mound in front of the Watchfire. This barrow mound should be of earth, and when it is finished, the following Sigils are scratched into the side:

Also, five Raven's feathers should be stood upright on top of the barrow. The herbs you need are, Celandine, Mugwort and Dwale. These are burnt in the quarter pots and on the Watchfire.

You also need a horn made from a cows horn, but a trumpet or bugle would probably suffice. The seasonal quarters are traced in the air, but if you wish to use the seasonal herbs in the pots, then add Herb Robert to it before putting in the herbs needed for the Summoning. This gives a total of five herbs in all being used.

There should be NOTHING in the middle of the Circle. No fire or cauldron, as you will need to mark on the ground the Atlantean Sun Temple Key or Sigil. For those not familiar with this Sigil, I have included a diagram a bit farther on in this chapter. The long leg of the Key should be towards the South quarter and the whole Sigil should nearly cover the ground within the Circle boundary of salt. The Key also, has its outline marked with salt.

All present stand within the three rings of the Key, facing North/North East. The Watchfire Guardian also should be standing within the Sigil. This Guardian needs to be a very strong and experienced Witch, as I have seen this person later on after the Evocation, "taken over" for a while by the "Otherworld Guardian".

After the Watchfire is alight, plenty of the three herbs should be put on it, and make sure that the herb pots are well stocked as well.

Once all are standing in the rings of the Sigil, the Circle Guardian then blows the horn or trumpet once in each quarter This is done by simply turning around within the rings to face in each direction. That is one of the reasons the Key has to be so large.

The first quarter faced is the East, then go deosil until North is reached.

After the horn has been blown in the East, everyone faces in that direction and calls in unison:"Vran! Vran Dusgadh! Vran! Dusgadh! Vran! Dusgadh! (this second word is pronounced "Doosch"). Then: Ar Vran Bhan Bhos! (pronounced Van vos). This is done in each of the quarters. You should not need to repeat this, but if you do, the horn should be blown each time also. The Otherworld Guardian appears in the North.

You will not have to dismiss the Guardian, he will go of his own accord. Afterwards, take everything down. Burn any herbs that are left, and scatter the salt from the Sun Temple Key, just scuffle it with your feet. Remove the barrow mound, and make sure you have obliterated the symbols. Once again, you will not want to do much afterwards, but you may want some wine.

I will repeat, that in particular with the Guardian, do not call him for a frivolous reason, even if he does not manifest (because of the aforementioned frivolity), you will find over the following weeks that he was aware of you.

Compared to the Otherworld Guardian, Herne the Hunter is a real pussy cat!

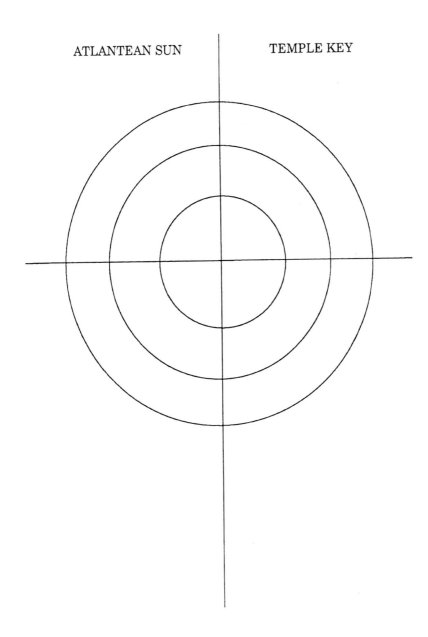

ATLANTEAN SUN   TEMPLE KEY

Mistletoe

When the Mistletoe is golden it is masculine and pertains to the Sun. When it is green and has berries on it, it is feminine and pertains to the Moon. However, the berries when crushed, produce a substance that resembles semen. So within the feminine, the masculine lies hidden. That is one of the Lesser Mysteries of the Druidic Path.

One of the Greater Mysteries is that the Mistletoe is the ONLY plant that changes its polarity on the seventh day of a New Moon, and on the twenty-eighth day of that same Moon. So the Mistletoe has a cycle exactly in tune with a woman's menstrual cycle. That is the Inner Mystery of the plant.

Of course, the Druids have their own ways of taking advantage of this cycle in their workings, using it together with the earth energy spirals, but these things cannot be written - at least not by me. Whether the Druids will ever set all their knowledge onto paper, I do not know, but at present the teaching is only in the time-honoured way of "mouth to ear".

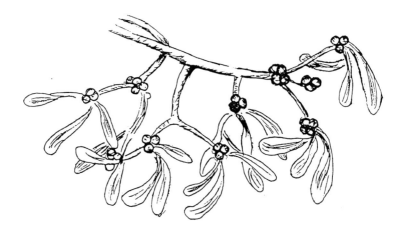

6 Pointed Star Dance

This dance is for raising energies of a particular type. The Star Dance has been used as the basis for some of the regional "Sword Dances" of the British Isles. These were enacted by men in winter, sometimes at the Winter Solstice. They also danced them on occasion at Spring or Summer Rites.

The energies produced are a darkish blue rising from the earth, and a rather subdued orange coming down from the sky. They mix together needless to say, in spirals.

The energy activated, is similar to the body's energies known in the East as "Chi". Some Martial Arts actually teach the pupils that these "Chi" energies are blue going up the limbs and trunk, and orange coming down. I will first explain this dance when it is performed as a Male Ritual:

When used for its winter purpose, five men only traced the steps, while a sixth played the music. The music was supplied by a fiddler or a man playing a penny whistle. The tune should be lively, and can be an old round dance tune, like "Sir Roger de Covelly", or a tune similar to an Irish jig.

One man stood at each point of the Star, the only person who would not move at all was the musician. He stood at either the top or bottom of the Star.

The music of course, is an integral part of the dance as the musician concentrates on visualising the musical notes weaving in and out of the other five's steps, and then being interwoven with them.

Nine Mens Morris has a somewhat similar underlying theme.

The purpose of the winter dance was to awaken and strengthen the earth's energies. It is done by the men dancing to the middle in a spiral, dancing the centre diamond shape, then returning to their places.

All the moves are made going deosil. Originally the men had long knives in their hands or wands, and when they got to the middle, they laid them in a pattern of a FIVE pointed star, stepped in and out of them in a particular way, and then returned to their places. Here is a diagram of the steps, followed by a description:

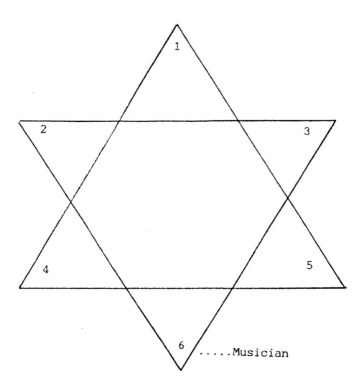

First of all the five dancers circle around the star deosil, then back to their original places.

Then, Number 1 moves round to number 4, then moves to the middle and dances into the very centre, in a rotating manner.

Number 2 circles past number 1's point at the top, on to 3 then 5, before also dancing to the middle in the same manner as number 1.

Number 3 goes round past 5,6 and 4, and then, as he reaches number 2's point, he also goes into the centre as the others have done.

Number 5 goes past number 4's point, halfway then to number 2, and then he goes into the middle rotating.

Number 4 sets off past number 2's point, also number 1's and number 3's, and then turns to the middle at number 5's point.

They all circle together once, then they all go across to the point of the diamond between the points numbers 4 and 2, up to number 1's point, across to the diamond point between numbers 3 and 5, down to number 6, then moving deosil, they go back to their own places.

When dancing towards the centre, they set off as simultaneously as possible.

The Star of course, was drawn on the ground with one of the usual materials; chalk, salt, mustard seeds, or quartz chips. Below, I have drawn a diagram to try and clarify the steps and directions of this rather complicated dance. I have included it, as there are so few Rituals nowadays that are solely for men.

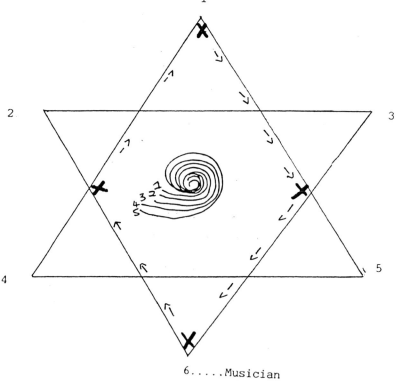

6.....Musician

 ......Diamond Points

I do feel sometimes that men get a bit left out in Ritual and this
should not be, as polarity in everything is the very bedrock of any
magical working.A fire can be laid in a hearth on a cold day, but
it won't do much warming without a match to ignite it! That is
what the male energy does, it ignites. But, there has to be the
female energy there TO ignite, or once again, not much is going
to happen.

The other version of the Six Pointed Star Dance, is really for a full Coven of thirteen. In this instance, it may be used for healing, or it CAN be used to prevent a person from harming or interfering in someone's life.

One should always be quite sure that a use of this kind is justified. The Ritual in any case will not harm the person, just keep them away.

If someone is being healed, they can stand in the middle of the Star. If they cannot be present, they are visualised as standing there,with all the energies entering into them, spiralling round, taking the illness away and destroying it.

If the energy is to be used to prevent someone from harming a Coven member or friend, then the negative person is visualised standing in the middle. The energies are seen enclosing them, turning into an orange star which still encloses them, turning into a blue star, which the person then becomes. The star then gets farther and farther away, smaller and smaller, until it turns into a dot and vanishes.

This dance is more complicated because of the number of people involved. But the musician may "Call" the dance, so that the dancers move into correct positions, a bit like the caller in a Square Dance in fact.

The music for this version is the *"Dilly Song"*, or *"Green Grow the Rushes O"*, as it is called nowadays. I will draw the diagram again, with the appropriate numbers on it, and explain the movements as clearly as possible.

There should be six men and six women dancers, and the Musician who was traditionally a man, although I see no reason why the musician could not be a woman, if one is available. On the diagram, the musician is called "1".

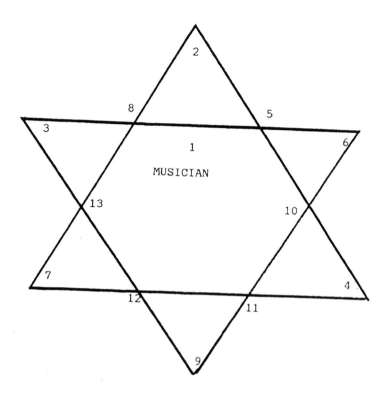

All except number 1 (the musician), circle twice deosil.
Then, numbers 5, 8, 10, 11, 12 and 13 move out to the
perimeter and go round once deosil.

Numbers: 2, 3, 4, 6, 7 and 9, dance to the middle, and go to
opposite places from where they started, - and pause.

Then: 7 goes to nine

4 goes to 2

2 goes to 7

3 goes to 4

9 goes to 6

6 goes to 3

After that, two women go to 3, two women go to 6 and another two women go to 9.

At the same time, two men go to 2, two more men go to 4, and another two men go to 7.

Each sex dances their own triangle, (made up of these numbers - see diagram), THREE TIMES.

If the energy is being used for a specific purpose, all now concentrate on the matter in hand.

The Musician directs the energies mentally, into the place they are meant for. If it is healing and the sick person is in the middle, the Musician stands just outside the Star at point two or nine. He still concentrates on directing the energies.

When casting the Circle to enclose this Star Dance pattern, the method used is the one described using wands or staves.

Working at the New Moon

New Moons can be a good time particularly in the Spring or Summer. You can try becoming acquainted with Nature Sprites of various kinds, for example. Summoning a Tree Sprite or Spirit is probably one of the easiest to attempt. Look at the Ogham Keys in chapter one to decide which tree sprite to try and Evoke. I give an example here so that you have some idea how to do it.

The Oak tree: this should be done between June 10th and July 7th.

If the New Moon does not coincide, this is still the best time to try, providing the Moon is WAXING.

With the Oak Wand, trace the appropriate Sigil at each quarter. Have sprays of oak leaves and acorns around the Circle. The oak leaves should be fresh and put into water, so if you are using a cauldron, put them in water in that. If not, a vase of some sort would be alright, and this can be placed in the North. Use dead oak branches on the fire, but do not try to start the fire with oak, as it is so very difficult to make it burn well.

The herbs should be Red Clover and Vervain, in addition to the Rosemary. That is because as the oak is more than one element and polarity, you need a bit of "mix" with the herbs as well, to make it easier to contact the Tree Sprite.

The Circle can be drawn as demonstrated overleaf, and this is the SYMBOL for oak, not to be confused with the SIGIL drawn in the quarters.

You call on the Tree Sprite using the old names for "Oak", either *"Derwen"*, (Welsh), or *"Duir"*, (Irish).

North

R.R.

The outlines of this symbol should of course be drawn in salt, or whatever psychic blocker you are using.

When the Rite is finished, burn all the oak leaves, acorns, arid any herbs you may have left, in the Circle before you leave. Or, you can leave the fresh oak leaves in their vase of water in the Circle, until they wither naturally when they can be burned.

The symbol shown below can be marked as large as the Circle itself, or you can make it smaller and put it in the middle of the Circle.

The Five Fold Calendar and the Thirteen Moons

Nov 12 - Dec 9   Hunting Moon or Month

Dec 10 - Jan 6   Knife Moon or Month

Jan 7 - Feb 3   Plough Moon or Month

Feb 4 - Mar 3   Primrose Moon or Month

Mar 4 - Mar 31   Axe Moon or Month

Apr 1 - Apr 28   Scythe Moon or Month

Apr 29 - May 26   Milk Bucket Moon or Month

May 27 - June 23   Stream Moon or Month

June 24 - Jul 21   Blackberry Moon or Month

Jul 22 - Aug 18   Grain Moon or Month

Aug 19 - Sept 15   Sickle Moon or Month

Sept 16 - Oct 13   Cider barrel Moon or Month

Oct 14 - Nov 11   Snail shell Moon or Month

Chapter Three

Murias

Underlying Fundamentals of Magical Working, and Related Matters

Apart from uniting polarities, which are really things we "do", there are things already "done" or "there".

So even without the knowledge of polarities and therefore the ability to use them, we are already working with the energies of earth and sky.

Cone and Vortex we engineer; the conical hat shown being worn by gnomes, witches and the like, is the "cone of power" above their heads, in the same way that a halo in a Christian picture, is really the top part of the Aura.

Earth energies along ley lines are active, but where they cross or intersect, spirals are formed, and these are much more potent. Some are extremely strong energy spirals and some less so. The ley lines circle the globe from North to South and from East to West. These form a grid over the Planet, but because of the flattening at each Pole, and the subsequent bulge around the Equator, this grid is formed not of squares, but of diamond shapes. There is a Celtic Ritual which calls for a "Diamond Working Area", which I will include in this chapter. If you go back to chapter one, and look at the Druidic symbols for Cone and Vortex, you will see that if placed together, they form a diamond shape.

The earth energy spirals are 3 half turns, either left handed spirals (female), or right handed and (male). Much of this old knowledge was in fairly general use until about the twelfth or thirteenth centuries, particularly in regard to weapons and their efficiency. For example:

> *"a pendulum of 27 inches vibrates at a rate of 72 in one minute. (An average heartbeat). The standard length of English arrows was 27 inches. If the arrow was fletched spirally it would travel in a corkscrew flight towards its target.*
>
> *An effective arrow will have a head angle of 38, a length of 27 inches, and an anti-clockwise spiral fletching. Such an arrow, by turning clockwise in the air will wind up the heart rate of its target by one beat per minute for each clockwise revolution, further more upon hitting its target it will cause clinical shock."*

(Extract from a paper given by a Senior Druid).

Angles are important in their effects. The angle of 6.4285714, will change the colours of the psychic centres (Chakras in Eastern terms), of the body.

Again I quote from the same Druidic paper: "This fact was known in ancient times and incorporated into the measurements of an Ankh, where the bottom angle is 6.4285714, to affect the colours and the side arms are 30 to affect the physical polarity"

The "psychic centres" are as I have said, similar to Eastern chakras, except that there are more of them in the Celtic system, and of course, the colours are different. I will include them at the end of this chapter, together with the Ogham correspondences.

To return to the energy spirals; there is a large spiral located at Stonehenge, and an equally important one at the Great Pyramid in Egypt. I have been told that because Egypt is so flat, the spiral at the Great Pyramid, is one of the few in Egypt. I have not checked this information however.

With regards to Stonehenge, I think one of the reasons many people for so long thought it was a Sun Temple, is because it was laid out according to the Kamea or Magical Square of the Sun. Not the numbers of the squares, but the PATTERN that is drawn from using those numbers. To clarify this information, I include the magical squares at the end of this chapter, and the patterns drawn from them.

Now on the surface, all this has not a lot to do with Witches generally, except that if it is possible to have a Circle on a spiral of earth energy, this assists greatly with charging the Circle up.

However there is more to it than that. It would seem that the Old Way - Witchcraft, was practiced by humans at least all over Britain and Europe, many thousands of years ago. Some of these very early people were the Megalith Builders. This is confirmed by the Druids who are quite emphatic that Stonehenge was not built by them - THEY DO NOT USE STONE CIRCLES - they only work among groves of trees! The Druids also confirm my remarks about WHO the Megalith builders were. They were those who worked the Dark Moon Cycle, and became known eventually in Britain, if not in Ireland, as the Wessex Tradition or Wessex Craft.

In Ireland, these Dark Moon people are known as the Fomorians. Later on, the Tradition that worked the Full Moon Cycle took over in Ireland, and these were the Tuatha de Danaan. In their legends of course, it says that the de Danaan gods conquered the gods of the Fomors, but that is poetic license. They were ALL THE SAME godforms or energies, but the Fomors worked with one aspect, the de Danaans another.

Now somewhere between the two, the Atlantean knowledge was passed on through the agency of the Druids. That the Druids adapted Stonehenge for use by themselves in addition to the Wessex people, there can be no doubt. The Druids work with

BOTH types of energy or godforms, their insistence on polarity and balance once again.

Also somewhere in these VERY far off times, there was a sort of merging of the Wessex and de Danaan Traditions, and this became known as the "Sussex Tradition", or "Sussex Craft".

So in these very early times, there were now three Traditions of Witchcraft, AND the Pagan Druids.

There is a theory that old George Pickingill was Sussex Craft, but as he died before the First World War, there is now no way of discovering whether this is in fact correct.

Now the Druids overlap to a certain extent with all these various teachings. As the Celts, if one goes back far enough, were taught their Magic and Craft, (Witchcraft is a CRAFT), which is really a philosophical way of life, on the Four Islands that I have mentioned earlier. So there has to be a certain amount of what I call "cross-pollination" between the various Traditions; particularly when we are considering a time-frame of thousands of years.

I have been told by those more learned than myself, that the British Alexandrian Tradition of Witchcraft, was set up so that the most promising, when they reached the so-called Third Degree, could then be taken into First Degree Sussex Craft, but I have never yet met an Alexandrian Witch, who knew any more than the information in the books on Alexandrian Craft, so I feel that this anecdote may be just wishful thinking.

Signals of Recognition

Hand Signals

There are quite a few of these, some no doubt will be familiar to the reader. One consisted of the hand being clenched into a fist, with the middle finger extended. This was usually a mans sign of recognition.

A feminine one was the first three fingers extended, the little finger being held down by the thumb, and these three extended fingers being laid in the palm of the other hand.

Another is a variation of the European "Sign of the Horns". This consisted of the little finger and THUMB being extended, the others folded down.

Finally, there was the making of a fist with the right hand, and enclosing it in the left.

Signs on the Ground

Most of these died out many years ago, at least as a serious means of passing on information, but the most common was the "Goosefoot", drawn to point in the direction that either the person had gone, or as a means of directing the "reader" which way to go.

GOOSEFOOT:

The signs that Gypsies used to make on people's front gates and sometimes on country lanes, had a lot in common with the Witchcraft signs. Also, the Gypsies custom of jumping the fire as part of their wedding ceremony, is the same as that for two Witches being joined.

Diamond Working Area

As I said previously, the Druid symbols for a cone and a vortex, together make a diamond shape.

CONE: VORTEX:

The diamond working area is based on the four islands of Finias, Falias, Murias and Gorias. When working in this way, the fifth island, the Sacred Isle, is the person using the place of working.

Mark out the diamond with salt, chalk etc, or dig a ditch and fill it with salt water. The four points of the diamond, should be visualised as Celtic Hill Forts. See Diagram on the next page:

The diamond working area is very complicated to set up. Traditionally, the diamond was marked out using multiples of the dimensions of the human hand; 9 inches for the long points, 4.5 inches for the short points. It is a measure of the age of this Ritual, that it is based on these simple dimensions. So the four Celtic hill forts are BETWEEN the compass points. The Ritual commences with you facing East.

You have to visualise standing in a small green diamond, which grows in size until it encompasses not only where you are, but the Circle, the whole Planet and eventually becomes the whole Universe.

While you are visualising this, you have to do what is known as "Setting the Wards".

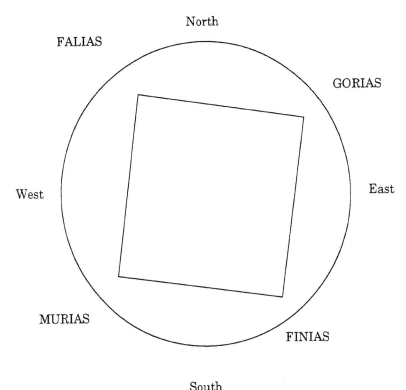

Still facing East, and the Universe still being a green diamond, you see a large, black, five petalled dog rose in front of you, but level with your eyes. The rose is made of Obsidian.

The centre of the rose is divided into a five by five grid. The centre is white and glows with an inner light.

You then declaim: *"From the Portals of Fire to the Portals of Earth, from the Portals of Air to the Portals of Water, from the place of the Fortress to the Mountains of Adamant, may this Sanctuary be established within the Black Rose, in the names of Oenghus, Bridig and Mannanan"*.

When you are doing the Portals, you have to turn to each COMPASS POINT, and draw the Sigil of Oenghus in them. You also visualise black Obsidian mountains all around the Circle, (although the green diamond is still the Universe),when saying "Mountains of Adamant"; also, re-affirm that the Black Rose is still there.

You can see how complex this is to set up. But it is well worth learning it.

The Sigil of Oenghus is as follows:

As I mentioned before, if you have a cauldron in the middle of the Circle, you can use its diameter to mark out the diamond.

When you have done all this, you can concentrate and see what happens, or you can do some Circle work within the diamond or you can dance and see what difference the diamond makes to the energies raised. You can use it in any way you wish. It does NOT need taking down again afterwards.

The main thing with Witchcraft is that it is a learning process, and grows, changes and expands all the time.

There are some bits of various Traditions in this book, but they all fit in very well together. The only time I reject anything, is if it does not work. If it works, use it. If you get little or no results after doing one particular thing several times over a period of months, then it is not worth the effort.

Sometimes effects build up over a period of weeks, but it is no good casting a Circle perhaps three weeks out of four, and at the end of a few months, you see, hear, and feel nothing more than on the first night that you started. it is a waste of time and effort. Witchcraft usually brings great non-material rewards to those who work it properly. That is one reason why Initiation by a genuine Witch from a valid Tradition is important. The Initiator "opens" the Initiate in various ways, so that they are able to be more receptive and can communicate with the unseen world more easily. Some very old Traditions actually imprint the Initiation in the Aura. I see it more as prising open a shell that has encased the person, including their eyes and ears.

I am now going to describe a little Ritual that can precede meditation, or can be used to gain entry to the Akashic records. I have not tried to use it in this way myself, as my past lives that I have seen, were all pretty dreary, boring stuff, not a hint or sign of having been some glamourous figure from the distant past for me!

You see a star lit night. In front of you is a large, tapering column of Obsidian, rising out of a pool of water. On top of the column is a silver, Lunar crescent lying on its back. Above the crescent between the "horns", is a large, flashing, violet star. The whole image is reflected in the water. Put up your arms to form the crescent shape, and synchronise your heartbeats to the flashing star. You can look directly at it the scene, or at the reflection in the water.

Once you synchronise your heartbeats, you should be able to go directly to the Akashic records. If you are using the scene for meditation, then visualise the scene you have chosen.

Of course, you can just do this visualisation, and wait and see what happens.

Something completely different, but included as an item of interest, is this old Saxon curse:

"I curse ye by a right line, a crooked line, a simple and a broken. By flame, by wind, by water, by a mass, by rain, by clay. By a flying thing, by a creeping thing, by a serpent. By an eye, by a hand, by a foot, by a crown, by a cross, by a sword and by a scourge, I curse thee.

HAADE, NIKADED, RAKEBEN, RIKA, RITA LI CA, TASARATH, MODECA, RABERT, TUTH, TUNCH."

I think these last words of which there are ten, are simply a form of counting in order to enforce the curse, a bit like tying knots in a cord. The reason I believe this is so, is that the words remind me of the strange method of counting sheep, used long ago by Sussex and Lincolnshire shepherds.

For those not familiar with this, I reproduce their counting methods here. First Sussex, numbers one to ten: One-erum, two-erum, cock-erum, shu-erum, seth-erum, shath-erum, winberry, wagtail, tarrydiddle, don. It seems very odd that the names of two Egyptian gods should be included in this counting. Now the Lincoln ones for one to twenty. Van, Tan, thethera, pethera, pimp, sethera, lethera, hovera, covera, dik, yan-a-dik, tan-a-dik, tethera-a-dik, pethera-a-dik, bumpit, yan-a-bumpit, tan- a-bumbit, tethera-bumpit, pethera-bumpit, figgit.

I will now explain about the Psychic Centres. There are eight of them and then the Aura, which is slightly different, but still included. The CROWN CENTRE is of course, just overhead. The THIRD EYE CENTRE is in the middle of the forehead. The THROAT CENTRE is naturally at the throat. The HEART CENTRE is in the middle of the breast. The SOLAR PLEXUS CENTRE is at the apex of the rib cage. The NAVEL CENTRE is the stomach. The LOIN CENTRE is in the genital area. The BASE CENTRE is at the feet. Around these Centres the Aura is seen as a great oval shape of pure white, enfolding the other Centres within it.

There are nine trees in Tree Ogham that apply to the Centres, although the Aura has a tree, it is viewed a little differently. This leaves five trees of the consonants over, and of course, the five vowel trees. The uses of these trees, not included, is one of the Greater Mysteries of Druidism, and I cannot write about them here.

A sidelight on the use of vowels is illustrated by the following anecdote: The first time I showed a Druid the vowels for the Five Festivals I was taught, (see chapter two page 39), in their order of Festival, he said instantly, "you can see what consonants should be written in, because then the five vowels will spell "Ceridwen's Bounty"". Which to him confirmed that time had not dimmed my memory, and I still had them in the right order. It also confirmed to me, that all the old systems must have had a common rootstock. The spelling referred to was of course, in Gaelic.

Now to return to the Psychic Centres and the various correspondences.

	Colour	**Tree Ogham**
Crown Centre:	Blue	Luis
3rd. Eye Centre:	Orange	Fearn
Throat Centre:	Violet	Willow
Heart Centre:	Turquoise	Hawthorn
Solar Plexus:	Deep Red	Holly
Navel Centre:	Light Red	Hazel
Loins Centre:	Green	Ivy
Base Centre:	Yellow	Reed or water Elder
Aura:	White	Oak

There is more detail of the trees etc, in a later section in this chapter entitled "Oghams".

I will return now to the "magical square" I spoke of earlier, which is the one I think that is the nearest we shall ever come to having a magical square for the Earth, in the same way that the squares for the Planets were worked out in the distant past. Here is the diagram, and overleaf I have given the full explanation of this rather enigmatic looking square:

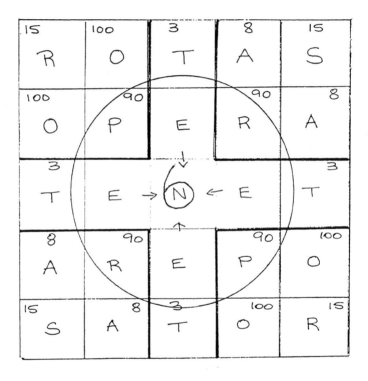

The numbers in the squares were not worked out by me, some one far cleverer than myself did this, but I have no idea how long ago it was. I have drawn the Celtic Cross in the Magical Square, so that I can demonstrate more easily what I am getting at.

The mathematical equation from this square, produces the total years in a Great Year; the grid is simply a graph of the Sun's passage.

Each letter represents a number as shown; the four "E's" in total are six, and these are shown collectively as the pivot. The four "E's" multiplied by the four "T's", total 72.

This figure multiplied by the sun's passage, i.e.: P.R.R.P (4x90)=25920, or the number of years in one Great Year.

If one then adds together: O+O+A+A+O+O+A+A, the sum is 432. If this is multiplied by the sum of the corner's, i.e. R+S+R+S=60, the answer is still 25920.

If one divides the Great Year by twelve one has the number of years in any particular Zodiacal Age, i.e. Age of Pisces, Age of Aquarius etc. 25920 divided by 12=2160.

The outside squares total each way 141, which reduces to 6, (1+4+1),the arms of the cross add to 6 each way, and of course the pivot is 6.

So we get three groups of six, which is 666, which is the number of the Sun's Magical Square.

One other point regarding this square is that it has a list of feminine numbers, when they are reduced to single digits. Column One:15+100+3+8+15=141=6. column Five is the same. Column Two: 100+90+90+8=288=18=9. Column Four is the same. The Diagonals: 15+90+90+15=210=3.

Now the significance of 3,6,9, for those who do not know, is that in many Celtic magical workings, particularly when using the bodies Psychic Centres, these numbers are most definitely feminine.

I had this peculiarity pointed out to me with the old (Basque?) chant which most Witches know:

Bagabi Lacha Bachabe

Lamac Cahi Achababe

Karellyos

Lamac Lamac Bachalyas

Cabahagy Sabalyos

Baryolos

Lagoz Atha Cabyolas

Samahac Atha Famalos

Hurrahya

Lines 3,6, and 9, are all single words.

You will find many instances of this group of numbers, for instance in the moon magical square, all three numbers are apparent. The Enneagram, where the triangle is viewed as being feminine, it is made up of these three numbers again.

There are gestures, sounds, colours, Sigils and musical notes which are part of the system using the Psychic Centres. However, when visualising these Centres, one line for each of the above may be recited.

With regard to the Magical Squares of the Planets; the designs that are taken from the squares, are arrived at by drawing lines from one number to another in a particular sequence. The Sun Square is the design layout for Stonehenge. if the pattern could be made large enough, and placed over Stonehenge, the two would match exactly.

The Great Pyramid is reputed to be based on the Mercury Square. There is purported to be a definite link magically between Stonehenge and the Great Pyramid.

Looking at the patterns, it would appear that Mars, Venus and the Moon, are based on the Saturn Square, and are just larger and more complicated versions of each other in progression. Similarly, Jupiter starts off the second type of pattern, followed by the Sun and finally Mercury.

There are diagrams for all these things at the end of the chapter together with some correspondences for the Psychic Centres.

Oghams

Because the Oghams are much more than a method of naming letters, (that are the basis of a complete magical system), they were very important to the Celts.There are 120 different kinds of Oghams, and Druids have to know them all!

Mannanan carried the Treasures of Britain in a craneskin bag. Arthur went to the Otherworld,(in the stories it says Ireland) to get back the Thirteen Treasures of Britain. They were the thirteen Ogham consonants. Oghams it is said, were carried in a skin bag. So the truth is obvious, and all these allegorical legends can be sorted out with a bit of patience - and knowledge!

This is the problem with old writings of course - that originally they were in Gaelic, which has now altered from its original form, and then been translated into English, mainly by Monks who didn't understand the hidden meanings anyway. The problem with having puns and riddles and plays on words, which is how they disguised what was really being said, is that so many Gaelic words are nothing like the English equivalent. That is how hidden meanings get lost or covered up.

An example is the Gaelic word "Mna", which means women. "Ban" means "woman", so there is not even a similarity between the singular and the plural. So if there was a pun hidden, or a play on words, the English translation would lose it altogether.

In the "Song of Amergin", there are thirteen statements which pertain to Ogham. Also, in Gaelic folklore any mention of shape-shifting usually refers to that person working their way through the Oghams, as a magical system. It is mainly referring to levels of Initiation. Amergin of course was a Druid, as were Taliesin, Mil, and many others. But I will go into all this and the Arthurian Myth Cycle, in the final chapter.

86

There are many more Oghams than those I include in this book, but I have listed the most general ones. Incidentally part of the "*Cad Goddeu*" - the Battle of the Trees, is concerned with Oghams.

One final snippet of interest: the "Charm of Making" from the film "*Excalibur*", is in Old Gaelic and is genuine.

Tree Name	Tree Ogham	Bird Ogham	Colour Ogham
Birch	Beth	Pheasant	White
Rowan	Luis	Duck	Floodwater Grey
Ash	Nion	Snipe	Clear as the wind
Alder	Fearn	Gull	Crimson
Willow	Saille	Hawk	Grass Green
Hawthorn	Huathe	Crow	Silver/Black
Oak	Duir	Wren	Charcoal
Holly	Tinne	Starling	Iron Grey
Hazel	Coll	Crane	Brown
Vine	Muin	Titmouse	Brown/Black
Ivy	Gort	Mute Swan	Blue Smoke
Reed	Ngetal	Goose	Sea Green
Elder	Ruis	Rook	Blood Red

A few final thoughts regarding the Oghams; the poem "The Spoils of Annwn", is primarily concerned with the Oghams, and Initiation, but it mainly takes place in the Otherworld, (which is of course, where the spiritual side of Initiation should have its effect), and that is why it has a certain dreamlike quality.

The Caers or Castles referred to in the poem are from "Castle Ogham". They also apply to the Psychic Centres of the body, but NOT in the order in which they are listed in the poem.

The "Spoils of Annwn" also refers to Initiation in a comparatively clear way, as it mentions, (but not in these words), the Druids standing in the Gorsedd, and also challenging and testing an Initiate.

The name "Gweir" in line three of the poem, is the same as "Gwydion". The names "Pwyll" and "Pryderi" in line four, mean "trouble" and "care" respectively.

The "Brindled Ox with the broad headband, whose yoke is seven-score handbreadths" or as it is translated in some books, "They know not the brindled ox, with his thick head band, and seven-score knobs on his collar"; refers to the constellation of Taurus, and the seven stars of the Pleiades, which are the "sevens" either the seven-score or the seven knobs.

It will be obvious by now, that while there is a wealth of information in old Celtic stuff, if has to be dug out before it makes any sense.

The lines that refer to the brindled ox are in verse five.

As a matter of interest, as this poem deals with Annwn, the Celtic Underworld, which is half of the Otherworld by the way, the poem would be concerned with vortex energy, which is female. There are six verses in the poem, and a total of thirty nine lines. So we have the female 3,6,9, combination yet again.

I will list here the names of the Caers, and their meanings in English.

CAER SIDI is the "Revolving Castle".

CAER PEDRYVAN is the "Four Cornered Castle"

CAER VEDWYD is the "Castle of Revelry"

CAER RIGOR is the "Kingly Castle"

CAER WYDYR is the "Glass Castle"

CAER GOLUD is the "Castle of Riches"

CAER VANDWY is the "Castle on High"

CAER OCHREN is the "Castle of the Sloping (or Shelving) Sides"

"Uffern" means the "cold place", so the lamp burning there (second verse), would be the Moon.

There are many bits of information in this very enigmatic piece of writing, but I feel that this will do for the present time.

4	9	2
3	5	7
8	1	6

SATURN

15(10)×3=45

4	14	15	1
9	7	6	12
5	11	10	8
16	2	3	13

JUPITER

34(17)×4=136

11	24	7	20	3
4	12	25	8	16
17	5	13	21	9
10	18	1	14	22
23	6	19	2	15

MARS

65(26)×5=325

6	32	4	3	35	1
31	5	33	34	2	36
30	8	28	27	11	26
7	29	9	10	26	12
24	14	22	21	17	19
13	23	15	16	20	18

SUN

111(37)×6=666

22	47	16	41	10	35	4
5	23	48	17	42	11	29
30	6	24	49	18	36	12
13	31	7	25	43	19	37
38	14	32	1	26	44	20
21	39	8	33	2	27	45
46	15	40	9	34	3	28

VENUS

175(50)×7=1225

8	58	59	5	4	62	63	1
49	15	14	52	53	11	10	56
41	23	22	44	45	19	18	48
32	34	35	29	28	38	39	25
40	26	27	37	36	30	31	33
17	47	46	20	21	43	42	24
9	55	54	12	13	51	50	16
64	2	3	61	60	6	7	57

MERCURY

260(65)×8=2080

37	79	29	70	21	62	13	54	5
6	38	79	30	71	22	63	14	46
47	7	39	30	31	72	23	55	15
15	48	3	40	31	32	64	24	56
57	17	49	9	41	73	33	65	25
26	58	18	50	1	42	74	34	66
67	27	59	10	51	2	43	75	35
36	68	19	60	11	52	3	44	76
77	28	69	20	61	12	53	4	45

MOON

369(82)×9=3321

90

Chapter Four

Gorias

Initiations

As this Tradition is based on a fivefold calendar, there are five Initiations.

The first one was really only a token of putting a child under the protection of the Goddess. It was usually done when the last bit of the baby's umbilical cord had come away.

First Initiation

A circlet was made of Hawthorn branches, interwoven with Rue and Rosemary, the piece of cord was fastened into this garland, and the whole thing was either floated down a river, thrown into the sea, or buried in a place with "Goddess" connections. The baby was also marked with the four elements, salt being substituted for earth.

Many, many years ago, the afterbirth was also buried, usually at the base of a standing stone. So the God form was involved as well. It must be noted, tthat even when I was having my babies, they were born at home in Britain, not in a hospital, so the parents had to dispose of the "gubbins".

This is what I call one of the "little magics", although it does count as the first of the Initiations. If a person was not marked by the Goddess soon after being born, then just before puberty a sort of oral examination would be carried out, to make sure that the youngster had some elementary knowledge and an understanding of it.

Second Initiation

So the Second Initiation took place at puberty. I would remind the reader that Witchcraft is old and earthy, although some young modern Witches have liked this second Initiation enough to decide to use it on their offspring at puberty. (One such called it "lovely").

What took place was this: The young person, and I will explain for a girl first, went to a senior Witch (who may have been her Mother), and said that she had commenced menstruating.

That night, regardless of the phase of the Moon, a Circle was put up and a fire was lit in the MIDDLE of the Circle. This fire was lit with wood kept especially for this purpose - Rowan, Hawthorn and Hazel. Rue was burnt in the herb pots, along with dried berries of the Hawthorn, and dried Rowan berries. The girl took with her the first article spoiled by the menstrual flow. This article was burned in the fire. As it burnt, the Witches danced around the Circle chanting:

> "Howell and Chion and Bav and Bru,
> charm for us as we call to you;
>
> We within the Circle's Might,
> call ye as Witness here, tonight".

I have spelled the names phonetically. This Call is done at the quarters, but not to each individually.

The fire was allowed to die down, some of the ash was put into a goblet of red wine, and one of the Witches, the girl's Mother if she was there, marked the girl on the forehead with the ash and wine mix.

Then the girl took the goblet, and poured a drop of the ashy wine into each quarter. One of the Witches took more of the ash and buried a bit in each quarter. Finally, the remains of the ash were put into a little leather drawstring bag, and this was given to the girl to keep.

This bag was a sort of Talisman, but in later years, if the girl wanted to perform some spell or charm that was very important to her, she would use a pinch of the ash.

For a boy, the Ritual was similar except semen was used not blood, and the woods burnt were Rowan, Vine and Ivy. Dried acorns were also put on the fire. The herbs were Rue, Mugwort and Celandine.

It is very difficult for people who live in cities, and come late to Craft, to realise that yes, it IS a way of life STILL, and yes, it HAS carried on secretly, as a Hidden Path should for countless generations. People who live in isolated country areas, and there are still many, do not change much over the years. In parts of Wales, the postman still delivers the mail on horseback, because the mountains are too awkward for a vehicle, and many parts of Europe, are still not mechanised on their farms. I live without the benefit of electricity, in what is supposed to be the most urbanised country in the world. I am five miles from a town of 800 people, and my nearest neighbour, (also sans the SEC), is nearly a mile away. All my children have been brought up in comparative isolation, either in Britain or here in Australia.

Now we have another generation growing up in the quiet greenness, my little granddaughter, who is six years old, has ridden a pony since she was two, who plays in my Circle, and floats leaves in the cauldron.

So although we are living at the end of the twentieth century, some things never change, we cannot keep to an ancient Path without trying to keep some of the traditional ways of living.

Of course Witchcraft has changed. It has to evolve and alter or it would become sterile. We no longer slaughter a man at the Harvest, we know it is not necessary and it is wrong. But we still mark the end of Harvest Time, or we would not be fulfilling our obligations to the Great Mother represented by our Planet, who, in spite of being poisoned, degraded and mutilated still manages to feed the majority of us.

Man is a superstitious being, maybe with good reason. Churchill ordered food to be given to the Tower Ravens during World War Two, as there is a legend that Britain will never be invaded while there are Ravens at the Tower of London. Of course the Ravens did stay, but whether they stopped us being invaded or not, who can say? But Sir Winston certainly hedged his bets on the issue.

Third Initiation

(First Adult One)

This Initiation would not be carried out until the person concerned was eighteen years old. Nowadays I think it a bit young, particularly for a boy, and that twenty is quite soon enough.

This Initiation was by way of being a re-birth, so a dolmen arch was used whenever possible. A Circle was cast, which included the dolmen within it, and this Ritual was always done on a waxing Moon, preferably the first quarter.

Casting the Circle was quite normal, with the seasonal Sigils and herbs used.

The Initiate had to be naked, and having fasted all day. They were led to the Circle blindfold, and taken to the Circle entrance, but outside the boundary. They were guided by voice into the Circle, and through the dolmen arch. On reaching the other side, the blindfold was removed, and the Initiate led to the fire, which was in the North East.

They were given a drink of warm wine, which had Sage, Nutmeg and Cinnamon in it.

Now all the Coven members fired questions at the Initiate as rapidly as possible. These questions pertained to the uses of Sigils, woods, herbs, all that kind of thing. The Initiate's working tools were already in the Circle, and questions were asked about these also. Their polarity for example, the energies in their construction, that kind of thing.

When everyone was satisfied that enough questions had been asked and answered, the new Witch was given robes which he/she had made themselves, and the cord to tie it, also made by them The Initiate was then taken to the four quarters, while the others declaimed:

"Here is .... (Witch name), now used for the first time, who is full in the knowledge of Earth and Water, Air and Fire, Iron and Wood, Stone and Wort! Harken when he/she calls ye, attend when he/she asks ye, give aid when he/she charms ye, in honour of the Great Mother".

Some of the burnt herbs and some of the fire ash were now given to the Initiate, who could add them to the bag with ash in it from the previous Initiation.

In addition to the Seasonal woods and herbs that were burnt, some of the same woods and herbs from the previous Initiation were also used in the fire and the herb pots.

After the presentation at the quarters, there would be a little celebration in the circle, and the new initiate could try a few small magics in the Circle, scrying in the cauldron water, or similar.

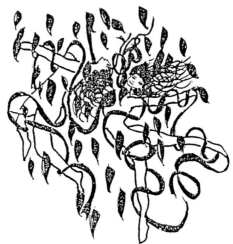

Fourth Initiation

The fourth Initiation, which would be at least a year and a day after the previous one, was of course, an Initiation of polarity.

These Initiations can be viewed as being concerned with one element for each.

The First, as an infant, is Earth.

The Second, at puberty, is Water.

The Third, in the Dolmen, is Air.

The Fourth, of polarity, is Fire.

The Fifth, which was optional, was connected with the Celtic Otherworld, and was of Spirit.

Here is the fourth one:

If a man, it was quite often carried out in daytime, particularly in summer.

For a man, the herbs are: Mugwort, or Nutmeg, or Wild Mustard, whichever was decided at the time, and Thyme, Fennel and Sage. The woods for the fire are: Oak, (small bits only as it does NOT burn well), Apple, Alder, Hawthorn and Willow.

In addition, Rowan berries were put on the fire, which was in the MIDDLE of the Circle.

For a woman, the herbs are: Yarrow, Hawthorn, Rue, Red Clover and Mullein.

The woods for the fire are: Elm, Oak, Rowan, Broom and Hazel. The Initiator erects the Circle, with the seasonal quarters. This was always done on a Waxing or Full Moon, even if a man, and taking place in daylight.

After the Circle is up, the Initiator stands in front of the Initiate and traces on their body, or just in front of it, the Sigils that are used in the quarters done with the staves.

No words are spoken, as concentration is needed.

This is to assist with making a person more " open " to knowledge that will come over a period of time, from the Otherworld.

I will explain where these symbols are drawn. They should be traced in this INSTANCE ONLY with the knife.

NONE of the words are recited.

Overhead the Sigil for the North:

On the chest and stomach, South Sigil:

On the thighs and legs, West Sigil:

Then over the whole body from about chest high down, the East Sigil:

While these Sigils are being traced, the Initiate should have some of the burning herbs near, so that the smoke goes over the Initiate.

After this tracing is done, the Initiate lays down head in the North, feet towards the South, and Ritual copulation takes place. While this is happening, the Initiator, prior to "going off" or leaving the body, places both hands on the Initiates head. This pushes more energy psychically into the Initiate.

This is a most difficult Initiation to do, because the Initiator needs to "come back" in time to use the life energies, by "catching" them as it were, and channelling their energy back into the Initiate.

In the East they have a way of doing of this, by using part of the lower spine of the Initiate, and giving one sharp stab with a thorn or similar. This will only work if the Initiate is a man, and I don't know of any Western system that employs it. I do think this Ritual is easier if the Initiator is a woman, but never having been a man, (at least that I can recall), I don't actually know. It IS very hard work however for the Initiator.

I have assumed that no one else will be present except the two people concerned, but if the Coven is very Pagan, they may have others there of course, and they also mentally give their energies to the two participants. It is usual nowadays, to have only the two participants present.

After this has been accomplished, and with the other Coven members now present, the man and woman concerned, (I am assuming that the Initiate is of the opposite sex to the Initiator) hold a goblet of wine between them, one clasping the bowl the other the stem.

If the Initiate is a woman, she declaims:

I have compassed a circle.
I have trod the Way that is not there.
I have been pierced by the knife that leaves no wound.
I have been crowned yet have no throne.
I have died yet still I live.
I shall heal the wound that none can see.

If the Initiate is a man, he declaims:

I have read the Signs that are not written.
I have swum in the sea which has no water.
I have drunk from the Cup that is always full.
I have followed the footprint that leaves no mark.
I have been crowned yet have no throne.
I have died yet still I live.
I shall heal the wound that none can see.

They each then take a mouthful of wine, and that completes the Rite.

Once again, the Initiate may take a small amount of ash from the fire and herb pots.

These Sigils that have been used, are themselves quite comprehensive. They can be used as the base for all manner of working, including postures during meditation, as it is now called.

I do receive criticism from "Old Craft" people for publishing old material, but I feel the time has come to broaden the base of passing on this old knowledge, instead of just mouth to ear. If I do not get TOO MUCH aggravation this time, I may later on publish all the work that the Sigils used are the base of; the Sigils are incredibly old and very potent.

Fifth Initiation

This Initiation is very different from the preceding ones in that it is optional, and it is solitary. In its way it is Shamanistic.

The would-be initiate from one New Moon to the next, ate nothing but fruit, vegetables and grains. Then fasted for the final twenty four hours. The Initiate chose the place to travel to for this Rite, but it had to be isolated and have magical associations.

Also, water had to be close by. I chose a place at one end of a gorge that was wild and rather dangerous to traverse. It had a waterfall at the far end with strong Goddess connections.

The Initiate was given dry wood to take, a goblet and a small cooking pot. Also some herbs.

On reaching the place the wood was used to light a fire, the pot filled with water and heated on the fire, with some of the herbs in the water to infuse. The herbs were also put on the fire. The infusion was put into the goblet and drunk.

The purpose of this Initiation was that the person went into a light trance state and travelled to find their "true" name.

Sometimes they found a sort of "totem" animal too.

The name that the Initiate is given or chooses when entering Craft is really their "public" Witch name. The one discovered in this Shamanistic way is their hidden or true name, which only one other person ever knows.

When this Rite is completed, the Witch, on arriving back home, goes to the most senior (in knowledge) Witch, and tells what transpired. From this can be deduced whether the initiation really happened or not. This is worked out from what had been encountered or seen and experienced. This senior Witch was the only one who was told the "secret" name. This also held clues as to the success or not of the Rite.

This hidden or true name would only be used if one was working very deeply and probably for oneself. Even then it was not uttered loudly, just whispered to oneself.

This Witch now made a "Shamans Bag", for want of a better phrase. The bits of herbs and ash from the other Initiations and some gathered from this last one also, were put still in the leather bag, inside the new one.

Any small stone or pebble or bit of wood that the Witch had seen at the place of the Fifth Rite and looked significant, would be put in the bag. After this it was a matter of what the Witch considered he/she would keep in it. It was a very private collection of things that could be used magically in the future.

Threading the Maze

(Shamanistic Initiation/Inner Planes Journey)

The Horns they gleam above the Gate
the crescent Moon shines through;
Stone Sentinel who doth guard the Way,
Is wreathed in mists and dew.
Green-White the Key to open wide
the Path that some may tread;
White blossoms - faded on their brow,
hearts filled with hope - and dread.
Both Cup and Wand their part must play,
bound in a Sacred Net;
Five points the Star enclosing all,
ere long - the Moon must set.
Who will pace the Perilous Trod,
that leads by thin hairs-breadth,
to all a heart is yearning for,
or perhaps to certain death?
But those who know the Signs and Keys,
who travel without fear,
will find the Path leads only
to all that they hold dear.
The Horns and Moon will bind their brows,
Glass Door will open wide,

all Mysteries are theirs to hold
enchanted by their Vows.
No Guardian will bar the Way,
No Watcher say them "No",

Antler and Hoof will bear them up,
on Old Ones Wain they'll go.
But faint of heart will not assay,
however great the guise,
for they will never find the Way,
Nor ever wrest the Prize

R. R.

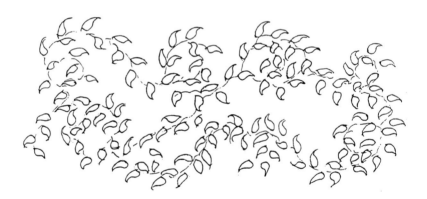

Some of the following come under the heading of what I term "little magics", they are more or less minor, but valid in their own way.

One of these is the old Anglo-Saxon "Nine Herbs Charm". according to the information about this charm in the British Museum it was a protection against almost everything from being overlooked to warding off poisonous snakes. However it is a bit of lore from many centuries ago, so I have listed the herbs here:

Nine Herbs Charm

Mugwort

Stime

Cockspur grass

Mayweed

Wergulu

Apple

Thyme

Fennel

Plantain

I have included it as it is written, but some of the names of the herbs are no longer in use, so here are the modern names for the few not familiar to day.

Stime is Watercress, Mayweed is Chamomile, and Wergulu is Nettle. Some old manuscripts put Chervil instead of Thyme, but I believe Thyme is the correct one.

It may be a "blind" of course, like calling "Herb Robert", "Dragons Blood", and "Vervain", "Graveyard Dust".

One other old "recipe" that never seems to be listed in its entirety is that of the "Fire of Azrael".

When it is mentioned in any book, only three woods are ever listed, when in fact it has NINE woods in its building.

So I list here all nine woods.

"The Fire of Azrael"

Rowan	Ash
Cedar	Elder
Yew	Sandalwood
Bay Laurel	Ivy
Juniper	

If it is not possible to obtain Sandalwood, then Horse Chestnut wood may be substituted.

When gathering herbs there are times when they are at their most powerful magically. It depends on what part of the herb is being used. Very early Spring if you are using the roots. If the leaf part is to be gathered then take them just as the new leaves are starting to open out.

For the flowers, the best time is when they are just changing from the bud stage. All herbs should be gathered in the early morning, and they should not really be cut with an iron knife, but it is very difficult nowadays to find a bronze one.

Gathering the roots should be done at Dark Moon time or on a Waning Moon. The leaves at a New Moon or one that is Waxing and the flowers at Full Moon. This all applies even though you will be gathering them in the daytime.

You should always bury something near the plant you have gathered. A small piece of bread is the most common item used. It is a way of thanking the plant. You should also try and prepare the plant by warning it of what you are going to do.

Never store plants in plastic or leave them in it at all. It drains the vitality from the plant. Gather them into a basket, and put them in jars to store. If you are going to dry them by hanging them up, put the tops in a paper bag to keep them dust free while drying, and store them in a dark cupboard. Even so, the virtue will have gone from the plant in about three months.

In the Welsh "Mabinogion", there is a woman made of flowers. There is also in old Celtic tales, a man made of fruits. Both flowers and fruits are nine in number. Home made wine can be made from the nine fruits and used in the Circle when matured. This is very good to use in this way, particularly at Samhain or Yule.

For those who may care to make these wines, I list the nine fruits here:

Plum	Quince
Wortleberry	Mulberry
Raspberry	Pear
Black Cherry	Crab Apple
White Cherry	

The flowers that the woman was made of can be dried as herbs and burned or the dried flowers can be scattered in the Circle, at Full Moons, Lady Day or Midsummer, so I will list these also:

Broom	Meadowsweet
Oak Blossom	Hawthorn
Primrose	White Daisies

Chestnut Blossom   Periwinkle

Nettle flowers White or Yellow

There are other "little magics" for making charms, spells, or talismans for oneself or others.

There are rhymes for involving earth based elementals of the four basic elements, to assist.

These chants are of course fairly "low key", but effective within their own sphere of working. So here is one chant for the four elements together:

"Hob and Lob and Will and Chlu

charm for us as we call to you,

work the spell with Circle's light,

send it spinning through the night.

Mix and meld the charm that's true,

Hob and Lob and Will and Chlu,

work the charm we send with you."

If you are working with a cauldron, you can change line three so that the chant says, "work the spell with cauldron's might," instead of "Circle's light".

This could also be used when working with cords, tying wishes into them, that sort of thing

This is where the idea of a "wise woman" came from, they were in the main Witches that concentrated on healing type herbs and these little magics, that so many people asked for.

108

There is nothing wrong with this, as the saying about Druids goes, "Every Druid is a Bard and an Ovate, but not every Bard and Ovate is a Druid"

Many Witches or Pagans in general, do not want to engage in big full-blown powerful Rituals. They are quite happy to gather or grow herbs, make healing possets and so forth from them, do some form of spiritual healing, and try to help the Planet. There must be many who only care for the more simple ways, that no one ever hears of, but who just quietly go about their business, and live a contented, peaceful existence, without many probably even being aware of what they do.

Chapter Five

Ceugant - Sacred Isle

In this final chapter 1 shall try and clarify the background that is the underlying structure - the framework, of Celtic Mystical Philosophy, whether of Witchcraft or the Druidic Path.

The main body of this information, (apart from that handed on orally), comes from the Irish *"Book of Invasions"*, and the *"Book of Ballymote"*, or the Welsh *"Barddas"* and *"Mabinogion"*.

Of these, the Irish works are older, the *"Mabinogion"* is derivative. It is an historical fact that the Irish invaded Wales, colonising it in part and that would be why there are so many similarities between the *"Book of Invasions"* and the Welsh *"Mabinogion"*. It is also an historical fact that the *"Lebor Gabala"* is the earlier work.

According to the pre-history of Ireland, the Fomors or Fomorians occupied Ireland for a considerable length of time, eventually being conquered by the Tuatha de Danaan.

In between these two events, there were the invaders called the Fir Bolg, but the main story of Ireland and its early people, is concerned with the Fomors and the de Danaan. After the de Danaan, the last people to conquer Ireland, were the Milesians under their leader, Mil.

Now while these people invaded and fought each other to the death, and were bitter enemies, they were obviously all originally of the same race. They could converse - they spoke the same language. The Fomors and the de Danaan intermarried. Their customs were similar, they all had a Druid class among the Wise Men or Shamans.

The general view is that all the invaders of Ireland, were originally Atlantean. They are the remnants and descendants of the three migrations that left Atlantis before it was submerged. These refugees, became known as the "Seed Bearers", in some regions of the British Isles.

It is these peoples who were taught on the Islands of Finias, Falias, Murias and Gorias, before they too were submerged, or removed from the Circles of the physical world. At one time there were seven islands of Atlantis, and each one had a Temple. The Sun Temple was one of these seven. There are names and symbols for all of them, some are incredibly ancient and are Fomorian, some are later and are de Danaan.

It may be that there were five inner isles and seven outer isles, that after the first catastrophe that struck Atlantis, there were five remaining for a while. I am not ure what time frame this all took place in, but it was probably years before the final tragedy, which is most likely the origin of the Biblical "Flood".

Most of the legends as I have already stated, are composed in the main of allegory. The name of "Mil" who led the Milesians, in one context means simply "Champion" or "Warrior". It is a TITLE rather than his given name.

This happens frequently throughout the Celtic legends. The name a person is called by, frequently describes their status, rather than being the name they were given in infancy.

The problems with trying to sort out Celtic antecedents is compounded by the fact that heroes were often given the names of gods, and that over a period of many hundreds of years in the distant past, the different groups which populated Ireland and overthrew those already there, had different names for the gods than their predecessors.

In addition, the de Danaan mythology states that their gods conquered the Fomor gods, when in fact, they simply connected with different sides of the same energy.

Then there is the problem of secrecy. According to authorities on the Celts in general and the Druids in particular, they spoke together in riddles, so that outsiders would not understand. Often I know, the Druids used a sign language with the Oghams or if speaking, used a mix of several Oghams together.

As the Welsh Triads say, "Hide the Secret! Guard the Secret! Disguise the Secret!" The Triads are the Druids great mnemonic device with everything in groups of three as the title suggests.

The late Robert Graves in his book, *"The White Goddess"*, (published by Faber & Faber 1961), mentions that the so-called "Battle of the Trees", was occasioned by, and he is obviously quoting, "a Lapwing, a White Roebuck, and a Whelp from Annwn".

Now the Battle of the Trees, is a competition of words- probably two Bards reciting their own poetical compositions, and one being judged the winner. The "Trees", are simply letters of the alphabet, in "Tree Ogham". The Lapwing, Roebuck and Hound, (Whelp is a word for a young dog), are three Oghams and they actually mean, "Hide the Secret! Guard the Secret! Disguise the Secret!"

It is told that three Cranes sat outside the Castle of Mannanan off the the coast of the Isle of Man, croaking at passers-by, "Do Not Enter - Keep Away - Pass By!" A variation on the "Secret" already mentioned. It is said that Mannanan kept the Thirteen Treasures of Britain in a craneskin bag, these Treasures being of course, the thirteen consonants of the Ogham.

I hope that the reader can now see how some of these very puzzling and enigmatic bits of writing, are actually clues to what is being concealed.

The Lapwing is from "Bird Ogham", the Roebuck and Whelp/Hound are from animal Ogham.

Robert Graves of course, was writing as an Academic not a Celtic Mystic, so while there is a great deal of very useful information in "The White Goddess", some of it is way off the mark.

As with the "Spoils of Annwn", not all is as it seems. One final example of how the Graves book must not be taken as definitive, occurs in a line he quotes from the old writings, which to him are arrant nonsense. The line is the second half of a question, and it asks, "How many worlds are there atop of two blunt spears?" What this question is asking, is how many generations of people would be fathered by just two men? The "two blunt spears", being two male phalli.

In the "Song of Amergin", he asks, "who but I know the secret of the unhewn dolmen?" This means he knows that to the Celts, the dolmen arch was symbolic of birth/life as well as death, because to be re-born, you must first die.

We now come to the reason that all these legends were written down and also the reason why so many of them, not least the Arthurian Myth Cycle, were garbled and "bowdlerised".

When Christianity finally came to the British Isles, the Druids agreed to assist the monks in writing down some of the epic stories. The Druids had offered to assist, because they knew it was the only way that the tales would not be lost. These sagas held truths and clues to truths, that those coming after would be able to sift out and interpret for themselves.

Of course all this was written by the monks guided by the Druids, many years after Arthur had fought his Last Battle. It was only by allowing a veneer of Christianity to cover the tales that they would survive. I believe it was Saint Augustine who told the monks when they were attempting to convert the British, "do not take their old beliefs away from them, but lay the new on top of the old".

That is why so many British churches are built on Pagan sites. This became evident after the bombing in the Second World War, when many churches particularly around London were destroyed. When the rubble was cleared away, Pagan altars were found that had been hidden underneath those of the Christian edifice, that had been built over the original temple.

So the Druids assisted the monks in order to preserve some of the esoteric knowledge. It is a commonly held belief that the Romans wiped out the Druids completely on the Isle of Mona. Well, there were certainly not many left alive, but the Romans did not ever invade Ireland, which was the heartland of the Druids.

Christianity nearly succeeded in doing to the Druids what the Romans did not manage, and that was to wipe them out. However, even the Christians did not quite succeed either. I expect everyone has heard the old legend of how Saint Patrick drove the snakes from Ireland, but it does not mean quite what it sounds like-it is allegory again.

The snake or serpent, was an emblem, an insignia in a way, of the Druids. So when it is said that Saint Patrick drove the snakes from Ireland, it simply means that he drove the Druids out. In fact, he did not even manage that, as many of them just went underground as it were, they went to earth, vanishing from the public eye, but still going about their business, unknown and unobserved, as they do to this day.

When Christianity came to the British Isles, its earliest form was the Celtic Church. (The present Pope has finally admitted and recognised officially, that the Celtic Church was the oldest form of Christianity in Britain). This early type of Christian belief, was still very much a mystery religion, and some Druids found it so similar to their own philosophy that they became christian. Much later when the established Church of Rome held sway, these early Celtic Christians were persecuted along with the Pagans as being heretics and non-believers.

Some Druids of course did not have anything to do with this new religion, and stayed obstinately Pagan. It is these Druids to whom I refer, and their successors over the past 1400 years or so. The Druids sometimes seen on television at Stonehenge for the Solstice and at the Welsh town of Llangollen for the familiar Eisteddfod, are a REVIVAL GROUP, formed last century, and are Christian.

So the Druidic philosophy of which a very small part is scattered throughout this book, has nothing in common WHATEVER, with the "Neo-Druids".

The Megalithic people who worked the Dark Moon Cycle, had nine deities. Those who came after them and worked the Full Moon Cycle, also had nine deities. Now these godforms are all parts of the same thing or energy, as I have already stated.

The "heavy" energies that the Megalith builders worked with, (using vortex) are on one side, or the "alter ego" of the "Light" energies, which are contacted using a cone, and this system was used by the successors of the Megalith builders. There is a whole, complex, magical system of working that was utilised by both these peoples.

I have not the room in this book to enlarge on all this, neither have I permission, from those who work these systems, to divulge them, at least not in such a public manner. If anyone cares to write to me, I will be happy to explain some of this type of working to them.

These deities then, will have more than one name each, and more than one type of personality, particularly when being written about as people rather than gods. The mythology has to be carefully sifted, in order to reach what is hidden, rather like finding a pearl in an oyster.

The prime key to Celtic philosophy is of course the Arthurian Myth Cycle, and that is why the Druids were so helpful when the monks decided to commit some of the legends to the written word. The re-telling of the tales had naturally, to be suitable for good Christians to read!

But they were PAGAN stories about Pagan people living in Pagan times. So the thin veneer of Christianity sits very uneasily on the saga of demonic parentage, (Merlin), adultery, (Arthur's parents and Arthur's Queen), incest, (Arthur and his half- sister). The list of Christian "sins", goes on and on!

In the time of Malory when no one had the slightest idea WHAT the stories were really about, the extra bit of sin - the Queen's adultery, was slipped in, to explain who knows what, but one could make a guess. All this "wrong-doing", makes one wonder WHY so many people were so interested in the stories, why the folk were so anxious they should not be forgotten? Not the Druids, but the ordinary people through the ages, who have been fascinated and puzzled by these old legends.

But if we return to the actual time-frame when these events took place, if one looks at the pre-Christian Celts, living in Tribes one can see quite clearly the underlying social system that the Arthurian Cycle is contemporary with.

The high born Celts in similar fashion to the Pharoahs of Egypt, practised incest in order to keep the royal blood lines pure. So there was nothing shocking about Arthur copulating with his half-sister unless one was viewing it through Christian or twentieth century eyes.

The rumour that Merlin was fathered by a demon and that Arthur was conceived because of a magical trick, is common among this type of myth. As all Magical children are born at the Winter Solstice, so all Magical or Supernatural children are not sure who their father was, or even if they had one at all. (Like the virgin birth of Jesus). The other thing the Celts had in common with the Pharoahs, was that they were Matriarchal - the heir inheriting through the MOTHER not the father. So in fact, who ones father was, did not matter as much as who ones mother was. This may be due in part to such Feasts as Beltinne, where it would have been very difficult no doubt to identify the father!

The copulation of Arthur with his sister, has all the appearance of Tantric Magic. I would say, and I am certain that I am correct, that this was an Initiatory Ritual on both sides. The only surprising fact about it is that a child was conceived. Now whether this was a deliberate act on the part of the girl, or whether it was due to magical inexperience I have no idea. The fact that a son was born, was fairly unimportant at the time, as he would have no claim on the throne. I will use the word throne although of course, it may well be the case, that it was only as a CHIEFTAINS son that he was regarded at the time, not as the son of a KING.

The monks of course, were transcribing these tales at a time when the world was Patriarchal, so the birth of a boy child would have seemed very significant to them, and they would automatically have assumed he would be the heir-apparent. The Druids would not have laboured the point of matriarchal inheritance, as it would most likely have led to unwanted discussions on topics the Druids would not have wanted to raise. The prime one being the Great Marriage with the land, which would have sealed the fitness of Arthur to be King.

This had nothing to do with his Ritual that concerned his sister, as I will explain. There are many stories of Arthur that mention that Gwynafar's father was troubled by a dragon in his land. This is another Druidic "blind". Any mention of a dragon, or dragon's blood, implies the blood of the Goddess within the family. We also read that Gwyanfar's father gave Arthur a great round table as a wedding present.

What all this means is that for Arthur to become King, he had to marry a girl with the sacred blood in her veins. This Gwynafar had, - as the dragon is mentioned. It was also sometimes referred to as "Dragon Might". So when Arthur married Gwynafar, the "great round table", that Arthur received as a wedding present, was the Island of Britain-Logres.

The name of Arthur's father, which should be "Uther BEN Dragon", NOT "Uther Pendragon", only signifies that the bearer of that name, was the father of Arthur.

The only way that a son of Arthur could inherit the throne, was by marrying a woman with the dragon blood. Often when a King died, his widow did indeed marry one of his children, if the mother was not herself. So Mordred wanting to marry Gwynafar is not so odd as it sounds, it was the only way he would have been entitled to succeed his father.

If Gwynafar had indeed given birth to a daughter, then the monks would not have found that very interesting, and the Druids would not have been very keen for it to be publicised, in case in those far off days, they had wanted a descendant of a daughter to challenge a Christian monarch. There is supposed to be one extant piece of writing that mentions a daughter, but I have never seen it.

As befitted a young man of his station, Arthur was taught by the Arch-Druid of Britain. That he was fostered in another noble family in his youth, is again, not strange. It was the custom for high-born Celts to foster their sons with other families, probably to prevent inter-tribal warfare. So both Arthur and in his turn Mordred, were following a custom. For a very long time, the secret of making weapons from iron was kept by the Druids. They were very Shamanistic in a lot of ways, and Shamans were nearly always Smiths, or to put it more correctly, Smiths were always Shamans. I think it was the late Professor Mircea Eliade who said, "Smiths and Shamans come out of the same basket".

It was because the average person was an illiterate peasant, who viewed the making of iron weapons with superstitious awe, that the mystique attached to Smiths was a normal - part of life at that time.

The ordinary people knew that it involved an anvil and a "stone", maybe even a meteorite, but how it became converted into a beautiful sword was an imponderable mystery.

So Arthur pulling the sword from the stone meant originally, that the people saw him take a stone, go with the Shaman/Druid/Blacksmith to where the anvil was kept. This would be well away one would assume from the tribal camp or village, and later when they reappeared, Arthur had turned the stone into a sword.

He had magically pulled a sword from a stone. By the time this was written down, the monks of course, were familiar with iron weapons as indeed was the whole population, so the only conclusion they could come to was that the sword was stuck fast in a stone. It had to be outside a church of course, to demonstrate that it was nothing Pagan or evil, (almost synonymous terms by this time), but the good Christian god that had let Arthur pull the sword from the stone.

Naturally, the Druids would not have enlightened the monks about the reasons for this puzzling tale, as even though the time had passed for iron making to be a secret Druid craft, they would not have wanted the monks to know. Neither would the monks have been interested in what they would probably have seen as "pagan Mumbo Jumbo".

Now we come to names; I have already explained how the name of the last invader of Ireland, Mil the Milesian, is also the word for "Champion" or "Warrior". The wailing Otherworld creature that some Irish families have to warn them of disaster, namely the Banshee, is actually nameless. The word banshee, means "woman of the Sidhe". (*Sidhe* is pronounced 'Shee'). The word "*Sidhe*" itself has evolved over the years to the point where it now has two meanings. It means the hillside, those same hillsides that Mil banished the de Danaans to live under, and now means also "the PEOPLE who dwell under the hill", now often also referred to as the "Sidhe". Irish Gaelic itself is a very difficult language. Some words can mean many things depending on the context and tense. Also, modern Irish is different from that of the original, as in the same way, modern English is completely different from that spoken in Geoffrey Chaucer's time.

Anyway, back to names; most people assume that the word "Merlin" or "Myrddin", is the given name of the man so called. This is not the case. Merlin or Myrddin is a TITLE. He was "The Merlin of Britain", the Arch-Druid in fact.

So when writers get all confused, and ask questions like, "who was Taliesin?" The answer is that he was one of a long line of Arch-Druids, of "The Merlins of Britain", in fact. He was also one of the three Merlins that lived during Arthur's time. This is why it seems that "Merlin" lived so long, there were three of them, each succeeding the previous one.

Similarly with the Lady of the Lake. Some writers say she was called "Nimue", some say she was called "Vivian". Both views are correct. The name of the Lady of the Lake in Arthur's day, was Vivian. Nimue is again a TITLE and means "exceedingly Great Lady".

Everyone knows how words get slurred and distorted over a period of time, so that even places no longer have the names that may sound how they did originally. An example of this is the epithet "bloody", which started out as "by the Lady" indicates its great age!).

Another is the archaic exclamation,"Zounds!" This started life as "God's wounds!".

The London district and Public House called in both instances the *"Elephant and Castle"*, is another example. This was originally, the *"Infanta of Castile"*.

The final example is the Irish/Gaelic, *"Ar N-Athair"*. *"Ar"* means "our", *"N"* is the linking sound, *"Athair"* which is pronounced a bit like "Ahur", means, when coupled with the preceding word, "Father". So *"Ar N-Athair"*, means "Our Father", in the sense of "Our Overlord", or "Our Chief", or "Our King".

Now if this phrase is quickened and slurred, it sounds very similar to the word "Arthur". I have been told by those who are authoritative in these matters, that my conclusions are correct. If you look at some of the early stories of Arthur, all the other characters sound Welsh or Irish. They have names like "Gawain", or "Geraint", "Bedivere", and so on. The name "Arthur" is nothing like any of these others at all, so what WAS "Arthur's" given name?

It was most certainly "Gwydion", sSometimes in later Welsh tales shown as "Gwion". In the "*Spoils of Annwn*", it is shown as "Gweir".

It is this same little Gwion or Gwydion, who was put to work by Cerridwen, stirring her magic cauldron. After a year three burning drops from the cauldron landed on Gwion's finger; he licked them off, and immediately had great knowledge. The fable goes on to say, that Cerridwen realising this, chased him to catch and kill him, but he fled away. He changed himself into a hare, she became a greyhound; he dived into the river and became a fish, she became an otter. He flew up in the air as a bird, she changed into a hawk. He became a grain of winnowed wheat on the floor, Cerridwen changed into a black hen and pecked him up. When she returned to her own shape, she was pregnant, and gave birth nine months later.

What all this really means is that Gwion or Gwydion received instruction from Cerridwen, or her human representative. He worked his way through the Oghams, as a complete magical system of learning, NOT just as letters, then underwent a Tantric Initiation with the Goddess, or again with her human counterpart. Subsequently he was "re-born" as a fully Initiated person. No doubt as a Druid, because his new name, was Taliesin.

However this new name may be another "blind", because Gwydion is mentioned in other tales that are of him when a mature adult. Then, he suddenly disappears, and Arthur is then written of. Many investigators of the *Mabinogion* and other contemporary writings, have puzzled over this abrupt switch, but they once again, were viewing it from an academic point of view, not an esoteric/Celtic slant. The reason for the change is obvious; Gwydion is now the King, and therefore addressed by his title, "Ar N-Athair" - Arthur.

Now we come to Arthur's Last Battle. It states that Arthur did not die of his wounds, but was taken away to be healed. This comes into the same category as Merlin being in an enchanted sleep. The Celts saw death as but, "the mid-point in a long life". This is because they believe in reincarnation.

What I think was being said is that the way of life and philosophy that both Arthur and Merlin symbolised, would go from the world but would one day maybe, be re-born. That the old view of living with one foot in the Otherworld, would return. That people once again, would live by the old values, revitalise the physical world, and appreciate its natural beauties once more.

I am aware that many people think that the "Age of Aquarius" will bring in a saner manner of living, with a renewed respect for other creatures that share this world with us.

The Druids also, see the turn of the century as a time of great hope, which is foretold through their knowledge of these matters.

Before I enlarge on this, I will explain that what I refer to as a Druid, is actually called a "Red Druid". Bards wear blue, Ovates wear green and Druids wear red. A Bard can study and become an Ovate, who in turn can become a Druid. It is from the ranks of red Druids that the Arch-Druid is chosen. The Arch-Druid being of course, "The Merlin of Britain".

One very senior red Druid, wrote an article about ten years or so ago, and it was published in an English magazine called "Quest". This venerable old man was ninety two when he wrote the article.

I have quoted his words in full below.

Crystals and the Grail

"We are experiencing in these times a considerable revival of interest in the legends of King Arthur and His time, and this is how it should be since the High One now treads the lands of men once more. So now we the faithful may part once more some of the veils that we cloaked His story in so long ago.

Of all the tales that have come down to common men from those dark times the one that strikes the most chords is probably the story of what is called the Holy Grail. What then is the Grail?

When first the world in which all things that are, was made, it was from, and in the reflection of, the Crystal Ring upon the Lady's hand that all things had their being. Then in later years when the Children of Danu sailed from the desolated lands of sunset to the green lands of mortal men they brought with them five treasures from the sunken lands that contained the essences of all things. They were a Sword, a Spear, a Cauldron, a Shield and a Stone patterned after the Lady's Ring.

Down through the ages until the coming of the High One, the treasures were kept. Then they were given into His hands since they were His in the undying lands, and when His work in mortal lands was done He rendered them back into the hands of the keepers who took them out of the circles of the world. Before He Himself passed beyond the mortal lands He passed His essence into the crystal that He and His father the Ever Young, should share a single life.

When the third of the Merlins of the High One's reign removed the stone through the great gateway, some of His essence also entered the stone so prodigious was the deed. Now since the crystal was patterned on the form of the Stone in the ring from which the world was made when it was removed from the circles of the world it became even as the Lady's Ring and its essence dwelt within all the crystal stones of mortal lands. Thus all the crystals contain the life of the Ever Young, the essence of the High One and the essence of the Third Merlin.

But the guardians of the way were far sighted, they looked down the course of years and saw the desolation of men's hearts and minds that was to be caused by those who styled themselves the followers of the pale Christ. So they changed the form of the tales of the High One to conform with the narrowness of men's minds but the essence of the tales they left the same, that the High One would ever live in the hearts of His people.

Now that men have had a chance to learn the folly of submitting to the tyranny of the followers of the pale Christ now that all His lands cry out once more for a King and a God to save them once again. The High One has heard the voice of His suffering people and come to their aid once more. For He is the King who has died for His land, and He is the son of the Ever Young, Lord of Love. He is the true King of the Hearts of all the Lady's children.

So the power of the crystals rises once again in all His lands, the shadow of the sickles rises above the five lands. The Raven banner shall fly once more beside the great banner of the Dragon and the Lady's Cross. The Great Falcon stretches his fiery pinions across the lands of mortals once again. For the last of the great prophecies are being fulfiled before our eyes, and lo, the Speaker for the birds is come. Harken to my voice for this is an age for Heroes not for carpenters."

This very enigmatic and thought provoking piece of writing ends with a kind of poem. I have not interpreted all of the poem, some of it remains a mystery to me. The article explains why there is so much interest in crystals all over the Western world, it is probably similar to a "race memory". I know all the explanation of the writing, but I hesitate to produce it in such a public manner, although any serious student of Celtic Lore, should be able to work it all out.

I have reproduced the poem that concludes this extremely thought provoking piece of writing.

Concluding lines of "*Crystals and The Grail*":

When the four crystal towers are one
When through the sea's gate shines the sun
When the wind meets fire and earth and sea
When silver grows upon the tree
When life glows within the stone
When returned is the throne
When the old powers are named once more
When open stands the oaken door
Then the Five Lands shall know their King
Once more His tale the bards shall sing
No longer hidden shall He be
Once more the powers of dark shall flee.

To return to the Arthurian Cycle; it is said that at the Last Battle, both sides agreed to parley. One knight however, saw a snake near his foot, and drew his sword to kill it. Someone from the other side, saw the sun glint on the sword blade, cried, "treachery!", and the battle commenced.

Now there are many things wrong with this bit of information. First of all, if they HAD been "knights", no snake could have bitten through a metal encased foot! However, we know that in Arthur's day, the Celts did not wear armour. BUT, if many hundreds of men were milling about in a field, there would not have been a snake for miles, the trampling of the feet and the horses moving about, would have sent a snake moving away as fast as it could go. There is no mention of the time of year, so it may not have been a time when snakes are about in Britain. After all, the only poisonous snake is an Adder, and they are in any case, very timid.

What are facts are the following: the Christians supported Mordred. Not on the battlefield, but covertly I believe. They were of the opinion that they stood a chance of converting Mordred to Christianity, and would have preferred him to an old dyed-in-the-wool Pagan such as Arthur, who would never have embraced Christianity. He was in his forties at this point.

The other fact is, that both sides had approached the Druids, and asked them to swell the ranks of fighting men. The Druids had a Martial Tradition among some members, and these Druids fought in a similar fashion to the Eastern type martial arts of today. I will expand on that farther on. Now the general view is, that on the day of the battle, the Druids came onto the field while the two sides were parleying, and allied themselves with Arthur's troops. Until that moment, no one knew whose side they would fight on - although I would imagine that Arthur knew!

When Mordred's troops saw this, one called out angrily, "treachery", and that was that. As I have said before, the use of the word "snake" or "serpent" is a "blind" for "Druid".

The "Lady's Banner" that Arthur carried into battle at the request of Gwynafar, instead of his Dragon Banner, was embroidered with the Celtic Cross. A symbol of the Goddess, NOT a Christian emblem concerned with Mary at all.

With regard to the Druids and their fighting techniques, if one reads the "Lebor Gabala" (the "Book of Invasions"), there is a passage that describes Nuada in his war chariot. It lists the types of weapons he had with him, and the number or quantity of each weapon in his chariot. They are identical in type and number, with those carried by an Oriental Ninja Warrior. This leads to the conclusion, that the weaponry came first from Atlantis and that the "Seed Bearers", in their scatterings across our world, taught many diverse subjects.

There is still one final mystery connected with Arthur, and that is concerned with Gwynafar. According to the majority of people who study the Myth Cycles there were THREE Gwynafar's. Now this may be the three aspects of the Goddess, it may be that it implies Gwynafar was the Goddess and not a human being at all. It may be that Arthur did in fact marry three times.

Gwynafar again, appears to be a TITLE rather than a personal name. It has the same interpretation as that of Ceridwen in some ways, in that they can both mean "White Lady", as "Blodeuwedd" - the woman made of flowers, means "Flower Face". Some old Welsh spellings of Gwynafar, also mean "Holy Essence", and this I think implies the supernatural quality of her.

The emphasis on "threes", may be due in part to the Druids almost obsessional attitude to Triads. Because it is the foundation on which all their philosophy is based, they DO like everything to be triadic. It is their principle of "active and passive with a reconciling neutral", which has of course brought this about.

So they see the three worlds of the Celts overlapping. These three worlds are demonstrated by three interlocking rings, which is also as much a symbol of the Druids as a serpent or a beehive.

I have included a diagram of the three rings. Our world is called "Abred", that of the Underworld is "Annwn", and this comprises half of the Otherworld, the other half being called "Gwynfed" or the "Blessed Realm", "Isles of the Blest", or "Avalon".

Avalon is NOT and never has been at Glastonbury. This confusion has arisen because there is reputed to be a doorway in the Tor which leads to the Otherworld - if you can find it and open it!

The Celts of course always considered it a simple matter to contact Otherworld beings, as they saw the worlds as being interrelated. It is more difficult nowadays, even for the Celts, the world has become so urbanised, and the majority of people do not live in the quiet of the countryside, but in large cities.

But no matter how much we may alter our way of life, no matter how materialistic the world becomes, the Otherworld is still there. To contact it satisfactorily though, you need to be out of doors, and have no sounds of so-called civilisation to intrude. It is also easier if one has some degree of Celtic blood, because the "Race Memory" is very strong among the Celts. I have found that those who practice some form of Paganism and have Celtic ancestry, are much more successful earlier in their use of Ritual which has a Celtic base. It is as if they were remembering rather than learning and being taught.

However as the Celts were the Fathers of Europe, travelling from the Balkans across the Continent and on into Britain, there are not so many people who have not got a bit of Celtic blood in their veins.

I have included in this chapter the "Song of Amergin" as it applies to the Oghams, (Amergin himself was a Druid), but first I will include a final piece from the "Cad Goddeu", which is concerned with Gwydion or little Gwion, also to be read of course, as "Arthur". It is a long statement, but has some very interesting calculations in it. There are nine sets of sentences or statements; all but one composed of three lines, the exception has six lines, so altogether we have the 3,6,9, combination. The total number of lines overall, is thirty.

I will explain some of its rather obscure statements after I have set down the lines, which are overleaf.

It does demonstrate the point I have been making, that all these old writings need to be sifted and interpreted, before what they are saying is revealed. Truly these old poems are a perfect example of "Hide the Secret! Guard the Secret! Disguise the Secret!"

Declamation of Gwion or Gwydion

"It is long since I was a herdsman
I travelled over the earth
before I became a learned person.
I know the light whose name is splendour
and the number of the ruling lights
that scatter rays of fire.
I know the star knowledge
of stars before the earth was made
whence I was born.
High above the deep
how many worlds there are
in myriads of secrets.
I know of the slaying of the boar
its appearing and disappearing
its knowledge of languages.
I am enriched
I am as learned as Math
my cassock is red all over.
My wreath is of red jewels
of gold is the border of my shield
with a golden jewel set in gold.
I am indulging in pleasure

out of the oppressive toil of the goldsmith
there has not been born one so good as I
or ever known
except Goronwy
from the dales of Edrywy.
Learned Druids
Prophesy ye of Arthur?
Or is it me they celebrate."

These statements and the *"Song of Amergin"* are not set out as clearly, as they are mixed in with other pieces of writing.

The speaker in this particular piece, Gwydion, claiming that his "cassock is red all over", implies that he is a red Druid, or a "Druid-Druid" one might say. Within the three Degrees of Bard, Ovate and Druid, are also three levels in each, therefore there are nine stages to becoming a Druid, which is why generally, it takes twenty years to become a Druid. Sometimes when being seen by people other than the Druids, red Druids will wear white, so as not to be identified. It is their belief that the red worn by Cardinals of the Christian church, and that worn by High Court judges, is based on the Druidic red.

The lines that mention the boar and his appearing and disappearing, are probably a reference to reincarnation, and refer to Arthur, who was symbolised by a boar in Cornwall.

The two dragons, one of red and one of gold, are connected with the two dragons of Druidry who are these two colours. They should not be confused with the "Dragon Blood", or the red dragon and the white which represent the Celts and the Saxons.

The light whose name is splendour and the number of the ruling lights, are references to the Psychic Centres of the body, taken in their widest context, which is as a complete magical system. The star knowledge would refer to the fact that Druids can and do use the stars as "Gateways", but I cannot explain this very complicated technique.

The final lines are said more or less "tongue in cheek", as prophesying of Gwydion is in fact prophesying about their High King which can be read of course as "Arthur".

For the rest, I think it mainly self explanatory.

There is another very old poem about the return of "Arthur", but not as old as the one just quoted. This particular one has had a date of 800 A.D. put on it, but I have been told that is probably incorrect! The author is also unknown, so the poems history remains an unsolved mystery. It is full of very valid imagery however, so I have included it. It is called, "Arthur - a Prophecy". Before I quote it though, I would like to touch on yet ANOTHER piece of poetry, which would appear to be earlier. At least, it is about the Old Gods of the Fomorians, the so-called Dark Gods.

It does seem strange that as we approach the end of the century, that all these old pieces of writing are starting to appear. The piece I will quote first is translated from the French by Michael Green, in his book,"Unicornis" published by Running Press, Philadelphia, in 1983.

The poem is called, "The Prophecy of the True Horn".

"Into darkness will I fade,
Into a night that Man has made,
But through that gloom shall gleam the Sun
When I am lost, and again am won.

Release! Release! I call to thee
In New Lands across the sea;
Let another, on narrow pathways come to me.

Furthest and highest
yet not beyond reach,
choose thou well a path that will teach
how the Sunken is raised
and Emptiness filled

and a wandering heart
can finally be stilled.

Seek the Great Stone! Mark it well with a sign,
that the one who shall follow
shall see it is mine,
and seeing, shall ponder and certainly know
as the Ancients have writ: As Above, So Below.

And I shall guard the Source of Greatness;
Waiting by a teardrop
from neither joy nor sorrow born,
in silver bound, beneath the ground,
I am the Spiral Horn."

Now the reference to the "spiral horn", may relate to the earth's energy spirals, also the Underworld is concerned with female energy as contact is through the vortex and silver is a Goddess metal. So it would be feasible to assume that the poem is concerned with the Old Gods.

The mention of a "new land across the sea", can be looked at as Ireland or the British Isles, if the speaker is an Atlantean figure, or it may imply a new land? in the context of what we call the "New World", which while it has mainly meant the Continent of America, could also mean Australia. There is a theory among some of the Celtic Path, that Australia will be very important in the "New Age", and that is why so many of us have come here.

Of the nine chthonic gods, three were viewed as being of major importance, and one of these was Crom. In Ireland there was a stone on a hill that represented him. In the tenth century, a poem was written about the worshipping of Crom and this poem indicates that the people were unwilling worshippers, who had to sacrifice their first-born infants to Crom in order to have food to eat. This would make him a harvest deity, which he was NOT.

One must bear in mind, that the poem was almost certainly written by a monk, with all the rules of the Roman Catholic church behind him; that Crom would have been worshipped at the Dark Moon time, with all that implies from a feminine point of view, and that Ritual copulation would no doubt have been part of the ceremonies.

The one line of this poem above all others that convinces me it concerns the Old chthonic Cods, is the line about "waiting by a teardrop". The Willow tree is an Underworld tree, a tree of the Dark Aspect of the Goddess, and its Sigil is a teardrop shape of water. This teardrop Sigil is a vital and integral part of a particular Ritual for contacting the Old, Dark Gods.

The Great Stone may be that Stone which is concerned with the Sacred Isle of the Celts, or it may be the "Stone of Fal", which Irish Kings were crowned on, and which came from the island of Falias.

The "Sunken is raised" may refer to these Old Gods resurfacing in the future should the times change. Crom could most certainly be described as being "from neither joy nor sorrow born".

The Druids in their insistence on balance and polarity work of course with both halves of the Otherworld. After all, you cannot have Ying without Yang to balance it. The Triadic view of the Druids, is an echo of the old teachings from Atlantis, of which the Druidic Path is the inheritor. This active, passive and reconciling neutral, is seen in the Qabbalistic "Middle Pillar" which has some of the old teachings, albeit watered down, abridged and adapted in its methods. I will have more on this later in the chapter.

Overleaf I have the old poem regarding Arthur. I have not written any explanation or commentary on it, as I feel that it is not necessary. However, if anyone wishes, they may write to me regarding it, particularly if it strikes a chord. I am fairly conversant with most of it, and its relevance to the Old Ways.

Arthur - a Prophecy

(Author and date unknown)

How mournful is the currach's cry
How dark and silent stands the hall
No hounds hunt across the sky
And silence on the mound doth fall.

Once where slept the Hosts of Light
Once where poets saw
Great lords clothed in armour bright
There's nothing anymore.

The Summer Lands now have no king
The Apple Isle has lost its lord
With grief the Tower of Glass doth ring
No great ships in the clouds are moored.

Now empty turns the Heavens Wain
Now no bones lie in hallowed grave
Now no great rider rides the plain
For vanished is the king most brave.

From all immortal lands he's passed
From all the realms of myth been torn
The looked-for time has come at last
In mortal lands a child is born.

The Three Worlds of the Celts

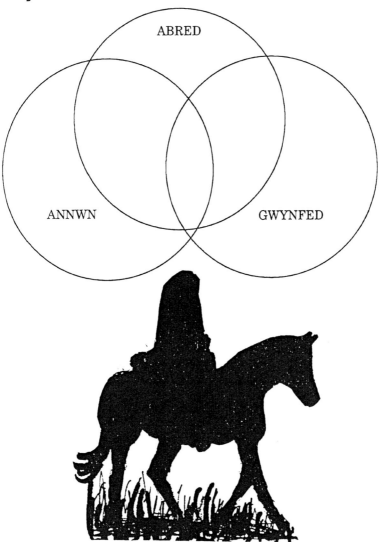

ABRED

ANNWN

GWYNFED

The Song of Amergín

(applied to the Oghams).

I am the wind that blows upon the sea.

I am an ocean wave.

I am a murmur of the surges.

I am seven battalions.

I am a strong bull.

I am an eagle on a rock.

I am a ray of the sun.

I am the most beautiful of herbs.

I am a courageous wild boar.

I am a salmon in the water.

I am a lake upon a plain.

I am a cunning artist.

I am a gigantic sword wielding champion.

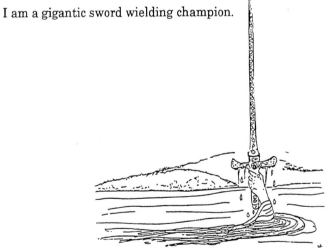

To discuss the Qabbalists "Tree of Life" in a book of Celtic/Druidic philosophy may seem rather bizarre, but it is not as far removed from the subject matter of this book as it may appear on the surface. Robert Wang in *"The Qabalistic Tarot"*, published by S.Weiser 1983, states that the "Tree of Life" has thirty two Paths, NOT counting the Sephirah. He quotes Crowley in support of this claim, saying that Crowley stated that only with 32 paths, could the Tree be worked properly.

In my view it is commonsense and I consider that the idea generally put forward that the ten Sephira are ten paths, is in itself a "blind". So is the view that there are only TEN Sephira, not eleven. The one known as "Daarth", is the only means of crossing the abyss on the Tree, and is actually a symbol for esoteric knowledge.

The Tree in its original form and its uses, goes back to Atlantis. The Druids use the Tree but not in the same form or manner as the Qabbalists. They use thirty two Paths, as it took thirty two strokes of Ogham to spell out the Nine Lettered Name of the Goddess and each stroke was one of the Paths.

If the Tree is drawn on paper, and the 32 Paths put in, then the Sephirah reduced to the size of dots, what one has, is a drawing of a crystal. The clue to the Tree is in its name; the "Tree of Life". Not a PERSONS life - but life itself as an abstract.

It proclaims to the world that it symbolises the basis of ALL life. Everything in this world, is ultimately energy, we know that, we also know that life is based one up from pure energy in crystalline structures.

Part of the complete magical system of the Druids and some other very old Celtic Traditions that I have mentioned earlier also incorporate the use of eleven Sephira, but again, in a completely different way to that of the Qabbalists.

If the Tree glyph is simplified even further, what is then arrived at, is three interlocking diamonds, the diamonds of the grid of ley line energies around the Planet, the diamond shapes that are part of the Druidic working.

I illustrate these two drawings of the Tree at the back of this book.

The Tree of Life pre-dates the Hebrews by many thousands of years. I have included these comments simply as a matter of interest.

To return now to Witchcraft of whatever Tradition! It is a method of aiding the Planet through energies applied in various ways, and it is a system that aids humans and other creatures by healing of various kinds, both physical and metaphysical.

Witchcraft is also a learning process and while we work it, we are enlightened in some ways at the same time.

Apart from these two main reasons for Witchcraft, it is also FUN! Any form of metaphysical philosophy, should bring joy and happiness to its adherents.

This is the great tragedy of Christianity, it is so gloomy dismal and negative. Full of "do nots", but very few "do's".

Witchcraft is full of laughter and humour, it should make one feel glad and uplifted. One of the reasons for following any kind of spiritual Path, is that it should instill in its followers a feeling of being complete, balanced, grounded and happy. We need this calm, balanced core to cope with life, particularly in today's world.

The more one works at Witchcraft, the easier it is to maintain inner balance. We all backslide now and again of course, we are only human, but Witchcraft is a very rewarding Path.

So I will now recount some of the experiences of myself and my friends in following this very old Way of Life.

But first a bit of background related to this Path we follow. The Witches Goddess and God, having been Invoked, Evoked and visualised for thousands of years, have form, built up no doubt by all those minds. They have become human in likeness, as many Witches can testify. Although the Godform is not wholly humanoid. However, when one has seen them, one knows they exist.

This is just one of the many reasons a Circle should be "worked" in as often as possible. A Circle constantly in use, by the same people, builds up within it a great deal of power that, over a period of time, never completely disappears.

That is why areas such as stone circles have great power within them even today. Avebury, Stonehenge, Callanish, are all examples that spring to mind.

A Witch friend of mine, Elizabeth, has a Circle that I sometimes work in. She has used it so much that it is difficult to remain on the everyday level when simply standing in it, even before any Ritual is commenced. She herself also has difficulty in remaining "here" when in her Circle. We have become a bit disoriented, not being able to find the North quarter straight away, in spite of the fact that Elizabeth has an Altar in the North. A couple of times she has quite involuntarily started to levitate - it does require a lot of concentration prior to working.

There is a saying that the Celtic Mysteries, "took shape in the flux of between states - twilight dew that was neither rain nor sea water, river or well water; the Sacred Mistletoe that was neither a plant or a tree."

Well, one certainly remembers all THAT when entering and working in Elizabeth's Circle!

I do not think there is anything which brings back the wonder and magic a child feels, as walking under the stars to a Circle that already has the fire burning and the herbs smoking up to the sky.

140

One of the most rewarding aspects of working with others is the empathy and rapport that builds up within the members of a Coven, even if it only consists of four or five people.

I remember one evening working with Elizabeth, just the two of us and, because of the particular work we were doing, great emphasis was placed on the colour green. We wore green robes, had green candles in the middle and so on. She and I were Casting the Circle together. She went round with myself a couple of paces behind her.

Now I knew that Elizabeth sees a blue-white light emanate from her knife tip as she casts. I always see gold. As we went round, I looked behind me to see what colour the boundary was. To my surprise it was green. Of course gold and blue together would make green, so, when we had finished the Casting I said to her, "You know you always see your Circle cast in blue" and before I could say any more she interrupted me with a grin and said, "Oh! I thought as we were working with green, I would do it green. Why, is that what you saw?"

We have found on many occasions that we "see" the same thing. It is very satisfying and also confirms that what one is doing, is working!

With my own Coven I find that we invariably see and feel in unison. This is when we are involved in the Rituals.

However working on the "Inner Planes" is usually a very personal experience, with personal knowledge and wisdom being gained. There have been exceptions even to that however, and sometimes two of us, or even more on one occasion, "met" when doing this type of meditation.

Empowerment by the Goddess at the Full Moon is the traditional way of receiving help and guidance for the group in general and sometimes for oneself as well. That is why it is so important for the woman who is bringing the Goddess into the Circle to be able to obtain the state of a light trance, mainly by having absolute quiet around her. The men Witches too, in touch with the God Force, often see and hear information of great value and interest for the Coven and for themselves.

The men in my Coven get quite diverse Godforms on occasion, and I am of the opinion that it is perhaps a link with a past life. One member who is extremely interested in Oriental philosophies and culture, sees a very European Antlered Godform, whereas my husband, who like myself is Anglo/Irish, sees a native American Shaman-like personage, with a headdress decorated with buffalo horns.

Animals are fascinated by Circles. I have several cats and two of them always come to the Circle, particularly at the Full Moon, and stay until the end. One always arrives early, well before the Circle is cast, but the oldest cat, who is the father of some of them, usually comes along just as we are about to put the Circle up. He always walks round to where we enter in the North East, and never comes or goes by any other route. He has lived with us in two houses, with of course two different Circles, but he has never varied where he enters it.

The liking cats have for Circles, is probably where the idea of a "familiar" came from in olden times, and was one more black mark against the unfortunates who were persecuted.

Incidentally, one of our horses has "grazing rights" in the paddock where my Circle is, but although his hoof marks could be seen around the outside of the Circle, he never ventured in, even if that was the only place where the grass was still growing. Being a "Goddess" animal, I always found this very odd. But, he did break his golden rule on one occasion, about three years after we had the Circle in that place.

We had done an Evocation of Herne, and the following day the horse, who is a stallion, walked into the Circle, squeezed himself between the cauldron and the quarter stone which is a very large piece of granite, and rolled in that area where Herne had appeared. I have an eighteen foot Circle, and the ground area was at most eight feet wide, taking the cauldron and the quarter stone into account. After he had rolled, he got up, went straight out and never went in there again. We could only assume that it was because Herne's mount is also a stallion, and our horse was establishing his ownership.

One other incident involving animals is a bit different, but quite interesting in its own way. Elizabeth had asked me to try and do an "Inner Planes" journey with her, as she wanted to go to Atlantis and see what the High Priestess wore around her neck. She had a theory that it acted like a levitating device, and that it was how they lifted stones to build the Pyramids and Stonehenge.

So one evening we decided to try this out. We sat at my dining table which is round. There were two male Witches, Elizabeth and myself. We all held a circle of copper wire, and visualised going down to Atlantis, as we thought that would be the best way. We decided to work for forty five minutes. How we would know when the time was up had not occurred to us, but I suppose one cannot think of everything!

I will describe part of it as it was quite interesting, although not a great success as you will see. Elizabeth and myself saw the same views, scenery and places, but that was the sum of our success. However, this is what we saw: A wharf by the sea. The sea blue and calm. The wharf was made of alabaster. We walked towards the West. A long paved way led from the wharf to the city. It was edged with pillars joined at the top in pairs of arches. It was warm, clean and peaceful. Great gates to the city which were open. The streets were full of people, who appeared unhurried and calm. They were all dressed in white robes, trimmed in gold.

We went into the Temple. This was very tall, with long windows set up high. Inside the Temple was a square throne which was white, it was set at the top of seven steps. A girl sat on the throne, with a veil across her face, like a little curtain.

I stepped up to look at her necklace. It appeared to be a huge, many faceted crystal, each facet being a different colour.

Before I could examine it in more detail, I was conscious of my dogs whining and making a fuss. I opened my eyes, and saw the dogs climbing all over Elizabeth, pawing her and licking her face. They had pushed the dining room door open. Elizabeth looked across the table at me and I glanced at my watch. It was exactly forty five minutes since we had started. So we assumed the dogs had been time keeping for us!

Incidentally, the men saw a quite different scene from the one that we did, and also different from each other. We always intended to try this again, but have not yet done so.

Inner Planes working, while fascinating and more often than not informative, is only a tool. It cannot replace the trials and tribulations of our physical world. It should never be used as escapism, and should never be used as an amusement. I think if it were, the returns would rapidly diminish.

Most of Elizabeth's experiences are of a very personal nature, being mainly concerned with her inner growth and wisdom, but her experiences at Full Moon she always writes up, mainly in poetry. Now Elizabeth is a very ordinary lady. She has had a hard life, she has seven children, is on her own with them and has been for many years. She has a basic but colourful vocabulary, and is on her own admittance not an extremely educated lady, but her poetry is incredible. She says that when she writes her poetry, it just flows out.

She is a warm, loving, caring person, who although not well off, keeps open house for any who call on her. Her main sphere of interest is in healing. She spends a great deal of time-and energy on this of ten with very dramatic results.

She also has a Coven and enjoys teaching others in the hope that they too will experience some of her feelings of deep fulfilment that has come to her from her many years on the Hidden Path.

She views her contact with the Goddess, as a personal communication with nature. I reproduce here, one of the poems she wrote at Full Moon. I have her permission to produce it here:

The Ageless One

Who was she?
She who sat beneath oaken tree
draped in silvery white sheaths of light;
Her throne of wood
hand carved it seemed,
glistened from her radiance.
The air, scented with unidentified fragrances,
whispered and swirled,
as a soft breeze danced around her.
Who was she?
she in all her loveliness and ageless beauty.
She who wore naught but light;
Not even a crown adorned her silken hair,
no flowers around her feet,
and her hands
bare of symbolic authorities.
When first I saw her
I thought it was I
as a reflection of hallucination.
But as I neared her threshold,
the thought diminished.
Spoke with her I did,
but of what eludes me.
Smilingly, her hand reached toward me,
and I felt the urge to kneel in adoration.
She took my hand in hers,
shyly I gazed into her eyes.
So young her face,
yet so old.
But then it seemed neither.
Who was she?
She who was ageless

I felt so much warmth,
compassion and endless love
flowing through her.
Then without speaking,
I heard her say,
"Would thou kneel before a flower,
a tree, or the sea,
or any other that I am?
Open thine eyes.
As I did,
I saw her standing before my Priest,
her hand upon his shoulder, saying,
"Arise. Cast aside thy words,
for I hear thy heart."
She turned to me
with a smile,
and was no more.
Who was she?

(*"The Ageless One"* copyright -"Elizabeth")

To me, that poem of Elizabeth's, and others that she has written, epitomise the true wonder of Empowerment by the Goddess at the Full Noon. Elizabeth travelled a long, hard road to reach the place she has in Witchcraft, but now she reaps a twofold prize. She has contact with the Lady, and she has the inspirational skills to put these experiences on paper in such a wonderful way.

Much of the work we do within a Circle is a learning process, for ourselves in particular, and this never stops. It is surprising but gratifying, how soon a Coven member who feels welcome and loved, learns what I call, "Flying by the seat of their pants". This is my rather inelegant description of being able to instinctively "know". Whether it is as a flash of insight, or a sudden conviction of what to do at a particular moment in working, whether healing, or in Ritual.

148

One male Witch I know, suddenly began receiving information from an entity, who both he and his Priestess saw, in Archaic Gaelic! They did not know what the language was, but wrote the words down phonetically, and gave them to me. I took them to an Irish friend, and between us we managed to translate it. This recipient, had no idea what the language was, or indeed, if it was a genuine language at all. Their expertise, while not insignificant before, has now progressed in leaps and bounds.

Rituals are a guideline. The ones given here, work very well, maybe because they have been done in this way for so long. But sometimes a Witch will find that they have altered something, not always consciously. Maybe for them, at the time, it will now work even better, because the clue came from their own subconscious. Quite often they are "remembering". So never become hidebound. We are all learning all the time. Some are going BACK to the Path, and the alterations they make, are because this was how they did it in some past life.

If the caring and camaraderie that exists in a Coven could be spread across the world, it would be of greater benefit to people in general than all of any Governments welfare and social services put together. Within Witchcraft, one gets closest to the old concept that prevailed - and still does to a certain extent, in village life. Where little groups assist and support each other, regardless of differences they may have in some areas of life.

There is hope that this attitude will eventually spread out to include more and more people in a caring and sharing environment. To me, the Old Ways are almost the last hope for us as we move towards the next century, and hopefully, those who should know are correct in their assumptions, that the New Age will be one of benefit to us all.

There is nothing I can call to mind that is as exciting, magical and uplifting, as a Coven meeting under a Waxing Moon. The fires, the smoke from herbs, the moonlight that shimmers down on the figures moving through an ancient Rite, as countless others have done through the ages.

The shape and age of people seem to fade into the background within a Circle, whether they are robed or not. All take on another persona from that of the everyday. The ordinary, daily irritations or even major worries of the mundane world fall away.

One is transported to another sphere of being. There have been periods in my life when I have not practiced "the Craft"; small children and many moves have been two reasons for my regrettable lapses. But always on the first night that I again take up my wand and cast the Circle, I know that I have come home again. The magic is always there. Sometimes one has to work harder at it, but always, always, the enchantment flows in, refreshing us all.

If there was one reason above all others why the Old Ways are to be preferred, it is because no followers of Paganism will fall into the trap of deifying a human and by so doing introduce religious bigotry into their lives.

Pagans recognise and acknowledge a prophet when one arises, but while they may see wisdom and enlightenment in that prophet's words, NEVER will they fall into the error of mistakenly perceiving something which is not there!

The main reason for this clearheadedness, is that Pagans generally are in touch with the Unseen World. They know for themselves the Dwellers in the Otherworld. They need no middlemen, no priest, Rabbi, or Imam, to interpret for them. Down through the ages Pagans have known those whose wisdom is greater than average. They are aware that these Masters have as THEIR teachers, Otherworld Beings, but Pagans NEVER CONFUSE THE TWO!

Merlin, Nimue, Arthur, all have Otherworld counterparts, but they are not the same. Pagans know this. Jesus, Buddha, Krishna all were great prophets and Seers, but they were totally human.

No Pagan starts a Holy War. No Pagan says, "My way is the ONLY WAY, my way is the RIGHT WAY". No Pagan reduces the Creator/Creatrix of us all to a petty being who will only recognise one tiny group of Rituals.

In fact, this One Supreme Being, who must obviously be Creator/Creatrix of ALL Universes, is most likely not even that which most "modern" religions address as "God". The Hebrew/Christian god, is most likely a god of our Solar System only, naturally both male and female, and therefore, the nearest approximation is that envisaged by Pagans - a Goddess and a God.

That the Triple-Aspected Goddess is valid, can be seen by the way that the church adopted a trinity. Making it all male was the ultimate absurdity, but the "sex-change" was obviously necessary to obliterate the Triple-Aspected Lady of the Pagans. BUT, we do not take up arms against them screaming, "Believe as we do-or die!" We of the Hidden Path, secure in ourselves and in our Goddess and God, can smile and continue with the ages old Rituals that bring us in close contact with the Lady and Her Lord, uplift our spirits, heal our sick, and hopefully stem the tide of destruction with which the "new religions" adherents are killing Mother Earth.

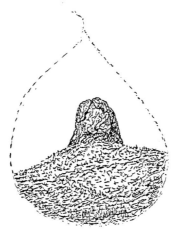

Full Moon Magic

Moonlight and shadows pattern the trees,
clear water sparkling - moved by breeze;
Shadowy figures pace out the green,
lanterns light glowing soft on the scene;
Of the cloaked figures circling - how many? - Thirteen.
Thirteen move round, blades held up on high,
hear them call! It echoes and vibrates high in the sky!
Lighted fires and herb pots, element called in,
the Circle shimmers - then starts to grow dim;
But only to those who are not taking part, for those in the
Circle - how fast beats their hearts!
This magical place now is not really "here",
it has become part of the world that is truly elsewhere.
From Otherworld Realms these folk now look forth,
and see Lord and Lady stand tall in the North.
O magical are earth, water, air and bright fire,
that accomplish all a heart may desire.
How dreary the lot of those not in tune,
with Old Ones and Magic and Might of the Moon.
For they'll never know the thrill of a glance,
from Lord and Lady as wildly we dance;
Earth, Planets and people all moving as one,
In our Mystical Circle, till dawn and the Sun,
comes up to remind us with bright light of day,
in the everyday world a part too we must play.
To try and prise open minds closed and shut tight,
to the magic of Circle, Dance, Charms and Moonlight.

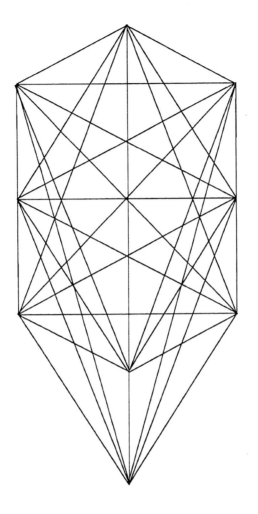

With the Sephirah virtually non-existent, it now becomes obvious
that this is a crystal, or a crystalline structure.

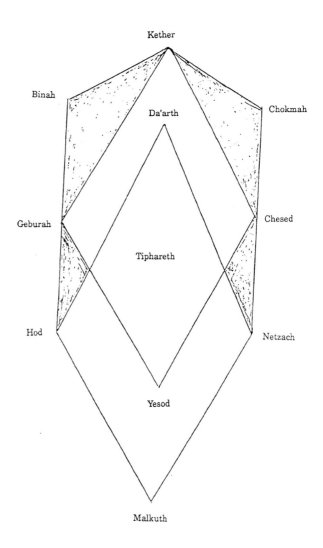

The three interlocking diamonds are highlighted by the
background shaded areas.

There are a couple of other ways one can look at this "Tree" glyph. The first is with pairs of the Trumps Major of the Tarot, two of each fitting each Sephira. These are placed according to their Titles, NOT their names. The other way is to place Celtic figures at each point. As shown here:

KETHER = GWYNFED

CHOKMAH = THE MERDDYN

BINAH = NIMUE

DAARTH = BRAN

CHESED = MODRON

GEBURAH = MABON

TIPHARETH = ABRED

HOD = GWNYAFAR

NETZACH = ARTHUR

YESOD = THE MOON

MALKUTH = ANNWN

In this way Tiphareth/Abred/our World, is where one can then reach all Realms through Archetypes and the Moon.

In order to clarify how the diagram overleaf was arrived at, I list the numbers of the cards and their places on the Tree overleaf:

KETHER:	Cards Zero and One.
CHOKMAH:	Cards Five and Twenty
BINAH:	Cards Nine and Twelve.
DAARTH:	Cards Two and Four.
CHESED:	Cards Eight and Ten.
GEBURAH:	Cards Eleven and Sixteen.
TIPHARETH:	Cards Six and Twenty One.
HOD:	Cards Three and Seven.
NETZACH:	Cards Seventeen and Nineteen.
YESOD:	Cards Thirteen and Eighteen.
MALKUTH:	Cards Fourteen and Fifteen.

Magus of Power -
Spirit of Ether

KETHER

Magus of the Voice
of Light - Spirit of
the Mighty Waters

BINAH

Magus of the Eternal
Gods - Spirit of the
Primal Fire

CHOKMAH

Son of the Morning -
Priestess of the Silver
Star

DA'ARTH

Lord of the Hosts of
the Mighty -
Daughter of the Lord
of Truth

GEBURAH

Lord of the Forces of
Life - Daughter of
the Flaming Sword

CHESED

Children of the Voice
Divine - Great One
of the Night of Time

TIPHARETH

Lord of the Triumph
of Light - Daughter
of the Mighty Ones

HOD

Child of the
Transformers - Rule
of Flux and Reflux

YESOD

Lord of the Fire of
the World - Daughter
of the Firmament

NETZACH

Lord of the Gates of
Matter - Daughter of
the Reconcilers

MALKUTH

Lament for the Fair Folk

Will the gladden golden times no more return again?
With the brave plaid colours and the green hills ringing;
Pure hearts uplifted at milk-white steed,
on his back Pendragon, to the wild pipes singing.

Old and straight the Elf-Path enchanted Druid Trod;
Stonehenge at the Solstice, Hawthorn snowy white.
Fierce and loyal Celtic Tribes who knew from the heart,
the Old Ones were the Wise Ones and their beliefs were right.

Ruby red was Hallowed Cup, white the Mistle's berry,
melded in together by ancient mystic lore;
Strength from the Oak Tree and brave Broom flower,
to weave charmed circlets the wise Priests wore.

Where now the true hearts, gallant, fey and strong
ancient Rites enacted under leafy bough?
Their spirit fled forever, gone from the land,
Earth weeps for the Old Ones that none remember now.

But some MUST remember the glory that has gone
whose spirits still are lifted, that come of ancient line;
Not everyone is heedless of the Magic in their veins,
some vestige of the Wisdom is in your eyes - and mine.

For they must be the losers whose heart no secrets hold
of heather-laden hillsides and the wild horns blowing,
so we hold our secrets fast and think on wondrous days,
of Logres and the Apple Isle and the great Moon glowing.

As throngs of singing Celt folk through the green lands rode,
Blue, green or red robes, down Old Paths coming;
To music of gaze-hound by rush and marshy fen,
welcoming the Old Ones, with golden harp strings strumming.

Index

Ivy, 26, 51, 81, 87, 93, 106

Jet, 32
Juniper, 106

Knife, 5, 8-9, 12, 15, 32, 35, 41,
   45-47, 70, 98, 100, 106, 141
Lady Day, 1, 22, 38-39, 41-43,
   107
Lady of the Lake, 120
Lady's Mantle, 41
Lament for the Fair Folk, 158
Logres, 28, 158
Loin Centre, 80
Lughnasad, 39

Mabinogion, 107, 110, 121
Magical Square, 73, 82-84
Man in Black, 7
Mannanan, 77, 86, 112
Mare's Tail, 51
Mayweed, 105
Meadowsweet, 107
Megalith, 73, 115
Mercury Square, 85
Merlin, 116, 120, 122-124, 150
Mil, 86, 110-111, 119
Milesians, 110-111
Mistletoe, 3, 58, 140
Mugwort, 24, 29, 41, 50, 54, 93,
   97, 105
Mulberry, 107
Mullein, 23, 97
Mute Swan, 26, 87

Nature Sprites, 67
Navel Centre, 80-81
Nettle, 105, 108
Nettle flowers, 108

Ng, 18
Nimue, 120, 150, 155
Nine Herbs Charm, 105
Nutmeg, 25, 95, 97

Oak, 5, 25, 29, 32, 41-42, 50-51,
   67, 69, 81, 87, 97-98, 107,
   158
Oak Blossom, 107
Obsidian, 77-79
Oenghus, 77-78
Ogham Keys, 3, 67
Oghams, 3, 22, 81, 86-87, 112,
   121, 128, 137

Pear, 107
Pendragon, 118, 158
Periwinkle, 108
Pheasant, 23, 87
Pickingill, George, 74
Plantain, 105
Plum, 107
Primrose, 70, 107
Psychic blocker, 5-6, 69

Quarters, 3, 6, 12, 16, 28-29, 42-
   44, 50-51, 54-55, 67, 92, 96,
   98
Quince, 107

Raspberry, 107
Red Clover, 67, 97
Rook, 27, 87
Rosemary, 25, 67, 91
Rowan, 23, 41, 50, 87, 92-93, 97-
   98, 106
Rubies, 32
Rue, 23, 41, 91-93, 97

FREE DETAILED CATALOGUE

A detailed illustrated catalogue is available on request, SAE or International Postal Coupon appreciated. Titles are available direct from Capall Bann, post free in the UK (cheque or PO with order) or from good bookshops and specialist outlets. Titles currently available include:

Animals, Mind Body Spirit & Folklore
Angels and Goddesses - Celtic Christianity & Paganism by Michael Howard
Arthur - The Legend Unveiled by C Johnson & E Lung
Auguries and Omens - The Magical Lore of Birds by Yvonne Aburrow
Book of the Veil The by Peter Paddon
Caer Sidhe - Celtic Astrology and Astronomy by Michael Bayley
Call of the Horned Piper by Nigel Jackson
Cats' Company by Ann Walker
Celtic Lore & Druidic Ritual by Rhiannon Ryall
Compleat Vampyre - The Vampyre Shaman: Werewolves & Witchery by Nigel Jackson
Crystal Clear - A Guide to Quartz Crystal by Jennifer Dent
Earth Dance - A Year of Pagan Rituals by Jan Brodie
Earth Harmony - Places of Power, Holiness and Healing by Nigel Pennick
Earth Magic by Margaret McArthur
Enchanted Forest - The Magical Lore of Trees by Yvonne Aburrow
Familiars - Animal Powers of Britain by Anna Franklin
Healing Homes by Jennifer Dent
Herbcraft - Shamanic & Ritual Use of Herbs by Susan Lavender & Anna Franklin
In Search of Herne the Hunter by Eric Fitch
Inner Space Workbook - Developing Counselling & Magical Skills Through the Tarot
Kecks, Keddles & Kesh by Michael Bayley
Living Tarot by Ann Walker
Magical Incenses and Perfumes by Jan Brodie
Magical Lore of Cats by Marion Davies
Magical Lore of Herbs by Marion Davies
Masks of Misrule - The Horned God & His Cult in Europe by Nigel Jackson
Mysteries of the Runes by Michael Howard
Oracle of Geomancy by Nigel Pennick
Patchwork of Magic by Julia Day
Pathworking - A Practical Book of Guided Meditations by Pete Jennings
Pickingill Papers - The Origins of Gardnerian Wicca by Michael Howard
Psychic Animals by Dennis Bardens
Psychic Self Defence - Real Solutions by Jan Brodie
Runic Astrology by Nigel Pennick
Sacred Animals by Gordon MacLellan
Sacred Grove - The Mysteries of the Forest by Yvonne Aburrow
Sacred Geometry by Nigel Pennick
Sacred Lore of Horses The by Marion Davies
Sacred Ring - Pagan Origins British Folk Festivals & Customs by Michael Howard
Seasonal Magic - Diary of a Village Witch by Paddy Slade
Secret Places of the Goddess by Philip Heselton
Talking to the Earth by Gordon Maclellan
Taming the Wolf - Full Moon Meditations by Steve Hounsome
The Goddess Year by Nigel Pennick & Helen Field
West Country Wicca by Rhiannon Ryall
Witches of Oz The by Matthew & Julia Phillips

Capall Bann is owned and run by people actively involved in many of the areas in which we publish. Our list is expanding rapidly so do contact us for details on the latest releases.

Capall Bann Publishing, Freshfields, Chieveley, Berks, RG20 8TF